# THE 100 GREATEST MOVIE STARS OF OUR TIME

# STAFF FOR THIS BOOK

Editor: **ELIZABETH SPORKIN**
Senior Editor: **RICHARD BURGHEIM**
Writers: **DANIELLE DUBIN, ELIZABETH O'BRIEN,
JOANNA POWELL, LISA RUSSELL, JENNIFER WULFF**
Art Director: **JANICE HOGAN**
Designer: **RONNIE BRANDWEIN-KEATS**
Picture Editor: **BRIAN BELOVITCH**
Imaging Specialist: **ROBERT ROSZKOWSKI**
Chief of Reporters: **RANDY VEST**
Researchers: **LAURA DOWNEY, DANIELLE DUBIN,
TOBY KAHN**
Copy Editors: **TOMMY DUNNE, LANCE KAPLAN**
Operations: **LISA BURNETT, GEORGE W. HILL,
JOHN SILVA, CYNTHIA VACCINA, PETER ZAMBOUROS**

**special thanks to:** Jane Bealer, Will Becker, Victoria
Boughton, Robert Britton, Joseph Cavalieri, Susan Chin,
Sal Covarrubias, Orpha Davis, Urbano DelValle, Maura
Foley, Sally Foster, Margery Frohlinger, Patricia Hustoo,
Salvador Lopez, Maddy Miller, Gregory Monfries,
Charles Nelson, Lillian Nici, Susan Radlauer, Deborah
Ratel, Mikema Reape, Patricia Rommeney, Annette
Rusin, Ann Tortorelli, Céline Wojtala, Patrick Yang

President: **ROB GURSHA**
Vice President, Branded Businesses: **DAVID ARFINE**
Executive Director, Marketing Services: **CAROL PITTARD**
Director, Retail & Special Sales: **TOM MIFSUD**
Director of Finance: **TRICIA GRIFFIN**
Marketing Director: **KENNETH MAEHLUM**
Prepress Manager: **EMILY RABIN**
Associate Product Manager: **SARA STUMPF**
Assistant Product Manager: **LINDA FRISBIE**

**special thanks to:** Suzanne DeBenedetto,
Robert Dente, Gina Di Meglio, Anne-Michelle Gallero,
Peter Harper, Natalie McCrea, Jessica McGrath,
Jonathan Polsky, Mary Jane Rigoroso, Steven
Sandonato, Bozena Szwagulinski, Niki Whelan

44

46

50

88

14

53

76

57

100

80

# contents

34

# ROLL 'EM

## From Hollywood's cast of thousands, these 100 superstars of today are larger than life onscreen and off

In 1974, the year that PEOPLE was born, so was Leonardo DiCaprio. Jack Nicholson launched his flight over the cuckoo's nest; a 10-year-old, Tatum O'Neal, won a Best Supporting Actress Oscar for *Paper Moon*; and the biggest grosser was *The Towering Inferno,* a disaster epic with a megacast ranging from Paul Newman to O.J. Simpson. The rest has been history, a shared history between the movies and a magazine. In this book, we showcase 100 favorites of the PEOPLE era, stars whose box office clout and dramatic, sometimes melodramatic, lives filled the screen and our imaginations.

Two of the book's luminaries were featured in the first issue of PEOPLE, which premiered shortly before the film *The Great Gatsby.* The adaptation disappointed critics but only enhanced the allure of its costars (right). Robert Redford continued as a dashing leading man, became a director and Hollywood elder statesman. Mia Farrow, a daughter of screen royalty, foreshadowed her soon-famous maternal instincts by shooting the role of Daisy Buchanan while pregnant. We celebrate these 100 one-of-a-kind originals, all legends of our time.

## MIA FARROW 3•4•74
She got cast in *Gatsby* after Ali MacGraw left her studio-boss hubby for Steve McQueen.

## GOLDIE HAWN 3•6•78
With a new baby and her 10th film (*Foul Play*), Hawn said, "Everything is copacetic."

## PAUL NEWMAN 6•25•79
At 54, the actor-turned-race-driver came in an amazing second at the 24-hour Le Mans.

## SLY STALLONE 6•21•82
"I did everything I could to crack the mold of being Rocky," he said after *III*.

## MICHAEL J. FOX 4•20•87
Fretting about his success, he mused, "I don't know if I've paid my dues or cheated."

## CLOSE & DOUGLAS 10•26•87
Close took the *Fatal* script to three shrinks to craft a psychological profile of her part.

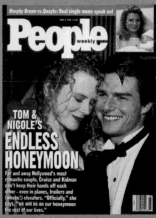

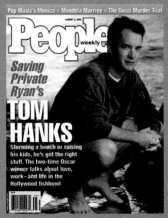

## KIDMAN & CRUISE 6•8•92
Nine years pre-split, Kidman said, "We will be on our honeymoon the rest of our lives."

## JULIA ROBERTS 7•7•97
Location pals noticed a warmer, more mature Roberts during *My Best Friend's Wedding*.

## TOM HANKS 8•3•98
After 24 films, the *Saving Private Ryan* star had won a rep as Hollywood's Mr. Nice.

**Gable and Grable are gone, but Hollywood glows on with these legends of our time**

# julia roberts

**born October 28, 1967**

From "incandescent" to "thousand-watt," "million-watt," "megawatt" and "blinding," more adjectives have probably been employed to define Julia Roberts's smile than GE has lightbulbs. It has also been called "the most profitable asset in modern cinema," although the actress once said it makes her look like "I have a hanger in my mouth." The third child of drama-coach parents in Smyrna, Georgia, she first dazzled audiences with that thesaurus-straining grin in 1988's *Mystic Pizza,* and she turned it up to nab Oscar nominations in *Steel Magnolias* and *Pretty Woman* within the next two years. Suddenly the coltish kid down the street with the hearty guffaw and buckets of charm was a major Hollywood player. She managed to weather lows like Steven Spielberg's *Hook* (during which she was dubbed "Tinkerhell") to become, by age 33, the first actress in history with films grossing more than $1 billion. And that was before her 2001 Best Actress Oscar for *Erin Brockovich.* Her growing fame enflamed the tabloids, which tagged Roberts as a commitment-phobe for her ricochet romances with Kiefer Sutherland, Dylan McDermott and Lyle Lovett (her husband of 21 months). She ended a four-year relationship with actor Benjamin Bratt in mid-2001 and began dating cameraman Danny Moder, 33. "She used to have a kind of deer-in-the-headlights quality," said *Pretty Woman* director Garry Marshall, summing up her evolution. "Now she stops the car."

# tom cruise

**born July 3, 1962**

He's the biggest male star of his generation, the swashbuckler with a blinding smile, the confident guy whose charisma, declared one writer, flashes "like a blowtorch." Whether piloting jets (*Top Gun*), hustling pool (*The Color of Money*) or racing stock cars (*Days of Thunder*), he built his rep playing egocentric hotshots who were at first humbled by a good woman only to rise to heroic heights of glory. Sure, it got to be familiar, but the formula made the famously focused actor ("I've never walked through anything") a $20-million-per-picture man. Along the way, he began to venture into more challenging roles, like the handicapped Viet vet in *Born on the Fourth of July,* the self-doubting sports agent in *Jerry Maguire* and the messianic sex guru in *Magnolia.* He nabbed Oscar nominations for all three. Cruise, said *Maguire* director Cameron Crowe, had now mastered "even richer, darker colors, along with light comedy as well." "Tom's at the top of his game," observed director Sydney Pollack, who acted with him in *Eyes Wide Shut,* the Stanley Kubrick psychosexual thriller. Now rising from the ashes of his divorce from Nicole Kidman, 35 (he shares custody of daughter Isabella, 9, and son Connor, 7), he began a new romance with his *Vanilla Sky* costar Penélope Cruz, 28. And even with all the media scrutiny, he concedes that being Tom Cruise is "the greatest job of all time. If you can't enjoy this, forget it."

# jane
# fonda

born December 21, 1937

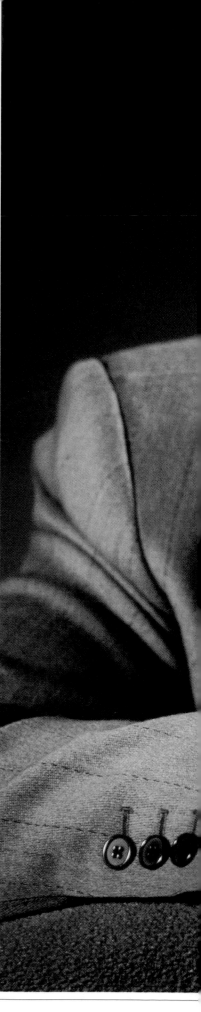

I've lived the most interesting life of anybody I know," Jane Fonda said at 50, neither boasting nor exaggerating. The only daughter of screen legend Henry Fonda purred into prominence as a sex kitten in *Barbarella,* directed by then-husband Roger Vadim, before transforming herself into a contentious tiger. She amassed seven Oscar nominations (winning two, for 1971's *Klute* and 1978's *Coming Home*), got pilloried as "Hanoi Jane" during Vietnam and built a multimillion-dollar aerobics-video empire. She then left movies to marry media mogul Ted Turner ("He's very much like my father," Fonda said, "with none of the bad parts") and became a devout Christian after their 2001 divorce. Staying in Atlanta, she's playing political activist and grandma, to Malcolm, son of daughter Vanessa Vadim (Fonda and her second husband, politician Tom Hayden, also have a son, Troy, and a daughter, Luana, whom they adopted as a teen in the mid-'80s). But old colleagues wish she'd return to the screen. Said Sally Field: "She is 'it,' as far as I'm concerned."

**y**ep, he got game. With enough range to go from Malcolm X to Shakespearean prince with lawyers and soldiers in between, Denzel Washington has become, according to *Pelican Brief* costar Julia Roberts, "the best actor of this generation." Other Academy members are obviously also impressed, this year giving him his fifth Oscar nomination and his first Best Actor win for his performance as a corrupt cop in *Training Day*. "This is the first time I've played a truly evil character," noted the actor. "That's not how Hollywood perceives me."

That's perhaps because the self-described family man, who has four children with his wife, Pauletta, 51, more often walks up the aisle of his West Angeles Pentecostal church than the red carpets of the premiere circuit. Shying away from the glitz doesn't mean he tires of the acclaim, though. Recalling his Best Supporting Actor Oscar win, for 1989's *Glory,* he said, "I remember the look on my mother's face. It was a heck of a thank-you card. She was just like, 'My baby. My baby's up there with the big boys.' " Indeed.

# denzel washington

**born December 28, 1954**

In a Hollywood crowded with giggly girls next door, she's the earnest girl at the library. For nearly all the years since baring her 3-year-old behind in the Coppertone ads, Jodie Foster has been the girl who gets the job done. "She's like one of those Budweiser horses—a Clydesdale," said Andy Tennant, her director in *Anna and the King*. "She looks like a Thoroughbred, but she's built for strength." A workhorse with a Yale degree, she wears her brains as easily as she does Armani. The principal breadwinner for her agent mother and three siblings, Foster took on a run of challenging, psychologically complex roles, from a preteen prostitute in *Taxi Driver* to her Oscar-winning turn as an FBI agent in *The Silence of the Lambs*. "The most true thing about me are the movies I make," admitted the famously guarded star, who now also directs. "They say so much about what I care about." Chief among those are sons Charlie, 3, and Kit, 10 months, whose fathers the single mom refuses to name. "I've lost any sense of competition," she has said, and works only every other year of late. "I make soups all weekend. I finally accomplished my finest ambition, which is to be the most boring person on earth."

# jodie foster

born November 19, 1962

# marlon brando

**born April 3, 1924**

He coulda simply been a contender, but Marlon Brando wound up beyond contention—and confoundingly contentious. Of his acting, Paul Newman marveled, "I have to break my ass to do what he can do with his eyes closed." Brando reigned over the 1950s, earning five Oscar nominations, starting with *A Streetcar Named Desire,* and first won as the embittered boxer in *On the Waterfront.* In 1973, supposedly washed up, he got a second for his embodiment of *The Godfather* but famously sent a Native American activist to represent him at the ceremony. Shuttling between a private Tahitian island and L.A., he had at least 11 children (five by his three ex-wives, three by his housekeeper and another three from affairs). In 1995 his daughter Cheyenne hanged herself, five years after her half brother Christian killed her boyfriend. Onscreen, Brando took on mostly embarrassing cameos at a reported $700,000 day rate. "It's been said I sold out," he noted. "But I knew what I was doing. I've never had any respect for Hollywood. It stands for greed, avarice, phoniness, crassness."

# tom hanks

**born July 9, 1956**

hoever said nice guys finish last never anticipated Tom Hanks. Over the past 14 years he's gone from enchantingly nice as a boy trapped in a man's body in *Big* to heartbreakingly nice as a lawyer dying of AIDS in *Philadelphia* (earning him his first Oscar) to heartwarmingly nice in *Forrest Gump* (source of his second Oscar). After being heroically nice in *Saving Private Ryan*, he has become a dedicated, effective activist for veterans' causes. "The man is as nice, as honest, as professional, as personal as he seems to be," assured *Gump* producer Steve Tisch. "His life is not an act." Which is not to say that it was always easy. His parents split when he was 5, and he spent an unsettled youth with his twice-remarried dad, a cook. As *Gump* costar Sally Field said, "He was a boy in search of a family." He finally found it with actress wife Rita Wilson, 45, and their two sons (he has another son and daughter from his first marriage). In Hollywood, Hanks has practically achieved the status of his idol, Jimmy Stewart. He has brought more than $2 billion to the box office and created a body of work that made him, at 45, the youngest recipient ever of the American Film Institute's life achievement award.

# robert redford

**born August 18, 1936**

He was dismissed by screenwriter William Goldman as "just another California blond—throw a stick at Malibu, you'll hit six of him," but once he saddled up in *Butch Cassidy and the Sundance Kid,* Robert Redford has been Hollywood's ultimate golden guy. "Redford's always had a great quality of incorruptible masculinity," observed Paul Newman, his costar in that 1969 classic. "His whole quality is American." He flavorfully plumbed the vagaries of our political system in *The Candidate* and *All the President's Men. The Natural* was his ballad to baseball, as well as an apt description of Redford, who won an Oscar for his directorial debut, 1980's Best Picture, *Ordinary People.* Founding the Sundance Film Festival earned him a second as "an inspiration to independent and innovative filmmakers everywhere." Divorced since 1985, this grandfather of four dates painter Sibylle Szaggars and lives in Utah but isn't fading into the sunset. "I'll run out of gas," said the Sundance King, "long before I run out of ideas."

you see his eyes no matter what he does," said pal Martha Stewart, a Connecticut neighbor. "He's so attractive that you just can't help liking him." Though Paul Newman constantly pooh-poohs his enduring sex appeal ("At my age," he quips, "I'm lucky to have a pulse"), he's one of those guys who just seems to get better as he gets older. If the industry had a Mount Rushmore instead of a Hollywood sign, Newman would be up there. The Method-trained tough guy of *Hud, Cool Hand Luke* and *The Hustler* grew more complex with time, winning a Best Actor Oscar (after six nominations) for *The Color of Money* in 1987. Increasingly devoted to family (five daughters, a son died) and good works, he has, with his wife of 44 years, actress Joanne Woodward, given away over $125 million since founding his philanthropic food company. He retired, reluctantly, from race-car driving at 70 but, despite 56 films in 48 years, is still reading scripts, seeking "one swan song. Something memorable."

# paul newman

**born January 26, 1925**

He's been famous longer than he's been alive," Dustin Hoffman said of his buddy Warren Beatty. An exaggeration, of course, but fame did seem to be Beatty's birthright, as the younger (by three years) brother of Shirley MacLaine. An alumnus of TV's *The Many Loves of Dobie Gillis*, he began a prodigious film career with 1961's *Splendor in the Grass* and earned 14 Oscar nominations (and a Best Director win for *Reds*). And his love life only extended his renown. Ex-fiancée Joan Collins described him as "insatiable" in her memoir. Woody Allen wanted to "be reincarnated as Warren Beatty's fingertips" and turned his famous pickup line "What's new, pussycat?" into a movie title. Beatty's performance as *Shampoo*'s hairdresser lothario echoed his real-life pursuit of Natalie Wood, Julie Christie, Diane Keaton and Madonna, to name just a very few. Then, in 1990, he met 21-years-younger *Bugsy* costar Annette Bening. The uxorious father of four now speaks of his life as having two parts: "Before Annette" and "With Annette." "Being an adolescent never got boring to me," Beatty said of his carousing days. "And that fortunately came to a conclusion, not a moment too soon."

# warren beatty

born March 30, 1937

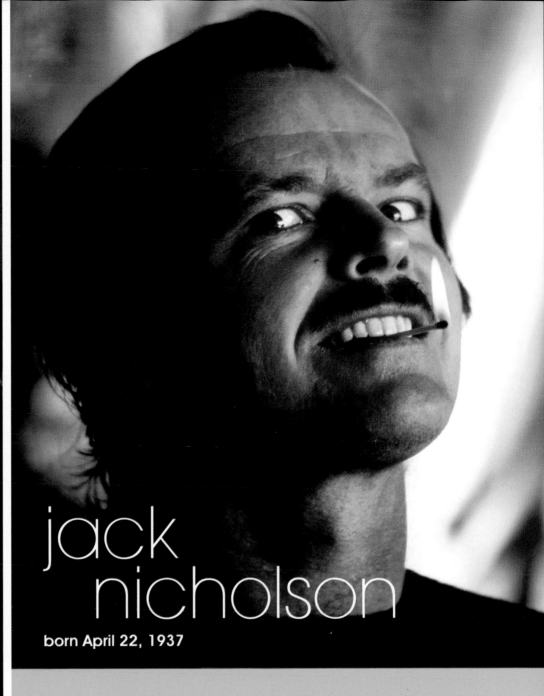

# jack
# nicholson
## born April 22, 1937

Heeeeere's Johnny! Whether axing his way through 1980's *The Shining* or preying on Gotham nine years later as *Batman*'s Joker, Jack Nicholson is the movies' Mr. Menace. With the pointy brows and that maniacal glare, he can scare an audience just by ordering a sandwich. "I'm attracted to devilish parts," he has said, and they've led to 11 nominations and three Oscars, not to mention a Kennedy Center lifetime achievement award. He wasn't honored for family values, though. Divorced since 1968 from actress Sandra Knight, with whom he had daughter Jennifer, 37, Nicholson has been the Jack of many hearts. Anjelica Huston, his *Prizzi's Honor* costar, ended their 17-year "understanding" in 1989, when he and actress Rebecca Broussard announced they were having a child; Lorraine, 12, and Raymond, 10, now live with her in Los Angeles, not far from Dad, who lately dated actress Lara Flynn Boyle. Said Nicholson, without apology: "I believe in living life to the hilt."

He's got a lopsided smile, an inch-long scar on his chin, and a nose he says has been broken three or four times. But despite those imperfections, "everybody is goo-goo-eyed over Harrison," assured *Working Girl* costar Melanie Griffith. With his breakthrough in *Star Wars* in 1977, flying the *Millennium Falcon* as Han Solo, the real-life pilot soared into the film firmament and has had many happy returns since, as a CIA agent (*Patriot Games*), an outlaw (*The Fugitive*) and a President (*Air Force One*), reeling in over $3 billion in ticket sales. "I'm like old shoes," he has explained. "I think the reason I'm still here is that I was never enough in fashion that I had to be replaced by something new."

Always a draw but never an It Boy, the ex-carpenter hit the nail on the head. Even as a "geezer" (by his own description), Ford has plenty of swing in his step. Recently agreeing to play rope-slinging academic turned adventurer Indiana Jones for the fourth time, the craggy-faced star said he felt "fitter now than when I was 35." His marriage to screenwriter Melissa Mathison has not withstood the same test of time. The couple, parents of son Malcolm, 15, and daughter Georgia, 12 (Ford also has two adult sons from his first marriage), separated in 2001 after 18 years. When he's not filming, Ford relaxes on his 800-acre Wyoming ranch and in the cockpit of his six-passenger Beech Bonanza. "It's become a big part of my life," he said of flying. "It's where I feel engaged and comfortable and free."

# harrison ford

born July 13, 1942

# BOMBSHELLS

**Loved by the camera, dogged by the tabloids, they stirred box office heat**

# halle berry

**born August 14, 1966**

o thoroughly distracting is Halle Berry's beauty that we almost didn't see it happening: After more than a decade in Hollywood, a Sparkly Ingenue became a Serious Actress. "I'm always fighting to prove that I'm not just the stereotype—that there's a brain behind my face," admitted the former model, who began building her case playing a crack addict in Spike Lee's 1991 *Jungle Fever.* She took the next step with her 2000 Emmy for the HBO biopic *Introducing Dorothy Dandridge.* This year came the clincher, when Berry gave an emotional acceptance speech as the first African-American to win the Best Actress Oscar. It was for her gritty, fiercely sexual performance in 2001's *Monster's Ball,* as a young widow involved with a racist death-row prison guard. "She was so open," marveled *Monster's* director Marc Forster, "so raw, vulnerable, committed, passionate." Raised in Ohio, the former cheerleader has been tested by a bitter 1997 divorce from baseball star David Justice and a 2000 car crash that resulted in a plea of no contest to leaving the scene of an accident. "Each time something happens in my life, good or bad, I'm getting stronger, I'm shedding that fragility," a wised-up Berry observed. In 2001, changing her press and luck, she wed singer Eric Benét, 35, and accepted a more frivolous offer: playing a Bond Girl (opposite Pierce Brosnan's 007). "I finally feel successful," she declared. "Like I'm part of the club."

# kim basinger

born December 8, 1953

A

ll of a sudden you're like a trunk going through an airport, covered in stickers," Kim Basinger once groused about how celebs get pigeonholed. "I've spent my life pulling off those stickers." Yet a couple of labels have stuck to her like tattoos, including sultry siren after her scorching refrigerator scene in *9½ Weeks* and free-spirited ditz after she headed up a partnership that in 1989 paid $20 million to buy the town of Braselton, Georgia, near her native Athens. (Within four years, following an unrelated lawsuit, she declared bankruptcy and was forced to sell her share.) At once outspoken and excruciatingly shy, she shrugged off a flattering comparison to Marilyn Monroe: "I'm stronger." But it was resemblance to another blonde icon—coolly glamorous '40s actress Veronica Lake—that landed her the breakthrough part of a pricey call girl in 1997's noir hit *L.A. Confidential,* as well as a sticker few ever expected: Oscar winner. "Kim's eccentric and mercurial, and such a contradiction," observed *Confidential* director Curtis Hanson. Alec Baldwin threw in the adjectives "absolutely maddeningly peculiar, exotic, lovely" before their 2001 separation. Currently she's content raising daughter Ireland, 6, crusading for animal rights and working sporadically. "I still haven't gotten to the core of who I am," she has admitted. "It's like I've got a garden, and it has a lot of weeds. Things need to be done to it, but it has a lot of potential to be reborn."

**H**e was famously shorter, but Nicole Kidman only really emerged from Tom Cruise's shadow when they split. After earning raves in 2001's deliciously creepy *The Others,* she got her first Oscar nomination in 2002 for a singing role in *Moulin Rouge* (who knew?) and now commands $10 million-plus per picture. "She has definitely entered the league where she can carry a movie," said Miramax's Bob Weinstein.

Born in Hawaii to a biochemist and his nurse wife and raised in Australia, Kidman dropped out of high school and made her U.S. splash in the 1989 stranded-at-sea thriller *Dead Calm.* That same year she auditioned with Cruise for their first collaboration, *Days of Thunder,* and married him on Christmas Eve, 1990. "I was lucky at 22," Kidman said, "that I met somebody who fascinated me, amazed me, who could keep me interested." A decade later they divorced, sharing a $350 million fortune and custody of their two children, Isabella, 9, and Connor, 7. The breakup, she conceded, was her personal nadir. "But creatively speaking, this is the best time of my life."

# nicole kidman

**born June 20, 1967**

# jessica lange

## born April 20, 1949

Jack Nicholson once called her "a delicate fawn crossed with a Buick"—which was a giant antelope leap from her launch as a starlet crossed with an ape. From that debut in the campy 1976 remake of *King Kong,* she took three years off to learn acting and went on to receive two Oscar nominations in a single year (1983)—Best Actress for *Frances* and Best Supporting Actress for *Tootsie,* the latter of which she won. "One of the things I love about Jessica is that she is one of the few actors who can really play a character with a secret. You always feel like there's something else going on," said Des McAnuff, her director in 1998's *Cousin Bette.* In truth, Lange is sort of her own best secret, more blessed in reviews than at the box office. Her second Oscar triumph, as a drunken housewife in 1994's *Blue Sky,* was seen, she joked, "maybe by 3,000 people." Accepting her low profile, Lange stepped back to raise her three kids—one with dance legend Mikhail Baryshnikov, the others with playwright-actor Sam Shepard, with whom she lives in her native Minnesota. She's galled about the limited choices at her age but has noted, "I look at the parts the 30-year-old actresses are doing, and I wouldn't want those roles either." All in all, she has concluded, "I'd have to say my life is great, knock wood. It's taken a long time to get there."

With 1998's *The Mask of Zorro,* this amply proportioned princess from Wales slashed her way to international stardom and provided Hollywood a throwback to such sexy sirens as Ava Gardner, Lana Turner and her own personal favorite, Rita Hayworth. "Catherine's glamor transcends time," proclaimed Joe Roth, who directed her in *America's Sweethearts.* "Catherine is very old-fashioned," explained Penny Rose, costume designer of her stylish thriller *Entrapment.* "She's not a belly-button-sticking-out and ring-through-her-nose type. She's a high-heels, full-makeup and beautiful-hair type." As Zeta-Jones put it, "I think I came out of the womb loving makeup." The daughter of a candy company official and a homemaker, she combines bourgeois bonhomie and regal beauty. In early 2000 she added the tingle of a May-December power romance, announcing her pregnancy and intention to wed Michael Douglas, who is 25 years her senior to the day. "I love the knowledge older men have," she confided. The couple teamed on the acclaimed drug drama *Traffic* and wed when son Dylan Michael was 3 months old. Her prenup agreement reportedly rewards her an additional $2.8 million for every year Zeta-Jones stays married, but don't expect this hardworking actress to disappear into domestic bliss. "She's always had this drive," her younger brother Lyndon Jones has observed. "When Catherine went onstage, it was like a tiger coming out in her."

# catherine zeta-jones

**born September 25, 1969**

# demi moore

born November 11, 1962

I'm very ambitious and very driven," Demi Moore once conceded. "I want stardom." She got it, thanks in part to a string of blockbusters, four nude magazine covers (one while seven months pregnant) and a power marriage to Bruce Willis (performed by Little Richard). Born a self-described "trailer-park kid" in New Mexico, Demetria Gene Guynes moved some 30 times before settling in L.A. She wound up estranged from her mother and at 18 began a brief marriage to musician Freddy Moore. By 20, she was playing Jackie Templeton on *General Hospital.* After leading the '80s Brat Pack (*St. Elmo's Fire* and *About Last Night*), she struck box office gold in 1990's *Ghost* and commanded a then-unprecedented $12.5 million for *Striptease* in 1996. Her 13-year marriage to Willis ended in 2000, and she took a break to be in Idaho with daughters Rumer, 13, Scout, 10, and Tallulah, 8, and martial-arts instructor boyfriend Oliver Whitcomb, 32. "She'll come back," assured movie exec Mike Medavoy. But when? "One of my goals," she once said, "is to build a loving relationship so that my children, as adults, will want to share their lives with me."

# sharon
# stone

**born March 10, 1958**

As the icy blonde seductress in the 1992 erotic thriller *Basic Instinct,* Sharon Stone became infamous overnight—with one naughty crossing of her legs. The stir earned millions for *Instinct* and established Stone as a calculated mix of beauty and bravado who would re-invent the Hollywood sex goddess. Over time the femme fatale also re-vealed underlying talent, earning an Oscar nomination as a drug-addled Mob wife in *Casino.* Meanwhile, her tart tongue and power plays struck terror in the hearts of the industry. "She didn't want to be taken as a dumb blonde," said *Action Jackson* director Craig Baxley. Indeed, Stone was born, she claims, with a genius IQ of 154 in Meadville, Pennsylvania, and couldn't wait to get out. By her early 20s, she'd landed a Charlie perfume ad and caught the eye of Woody Allen, who cast her in *Stardust Memories.* Married briefly to TV producer Michael Greenburg, Stone dined out on her man-eater image, dismissing ex-beau Dwight Yoakam as a "dirt sandwich" and reportedly returning fiancé Bob Wagner's ring by express mail. She eventually found love in the brawny arms of *San Francisco Chronicle* executive editor Phil Bronstein. Wed on Valentine's Day, 1998, the couple adopted a son, Roan, two years later. Out of the blue, in 2001, the resilient actress suffered a life-threatening brain hemorrhage—and survived without complications. Lucky? Definitely. But talk about a will of Stone.

# michelle pfeiffer

**born April 29, 1958**

ou can't talk about Michelle Pfeiffer without talking about that face. "Unbelievably beautiful," said Rob Reiner, who directed her in *The Story of Us*. "She has become more luminous the more mature she has become," concurred *Deep End of the Ocean* author Jacquelyn Mitchard. Before Pfeiffer ascended to Hollywood's screen-goddess pantheon, she was a golden girl from the beaches of Southern California, Miss Orange County of 1978 and "The Bombshell" on TV's sophomoric *Delta House*. She finally broke from type in 1983 as a coke-snorting moll in Brian De Palma's remake of *Scarface*. As further evidence of her range and ambition, she sizzled as the sultry chanteuse in *The Fabulous Baker Boys* and ventured into the artsier *The Age of Innocence* and *Dangerous Liaisons*, collecting three Oscar nominations along the way. Offscreen, life was bumpier. After a nine-year marriage to actor Peter Horton and a three-year relationship with actor Fisher Stevens, Pfeiffer decided she didn't need a man to become a mom and adopted Claudia Rose, now 9, in 1993. That same year she met and married David E. Kelley, 46, prodigious producer of TV's *Ally McBeal* and *The Practice*, and nine months later gave birth to John Henry, 7. The result, she has said, is a happy lady: "You can definitely see it on my face." That face.

# HEARTTHRO

## Behind their matinee-idol mugs lurks a boyish, modern, crowd-pleasing mischief

# george clooney

**born May 6, 1961**

is 2000 film about a fishing-boat disaster, *The Perfect Storm,* confirmed for movie fans that George Clooney was the perfect catch. Viewers of the TV smash *ER* had already fallen six years earlier for those crinkly puppy-dog eyes, that silvery please-touch stubble and his Cary Grant-meets-Clark Gable blend of charm and sex appeal. "It's hysterical to watch what happens to women when they're near George," said Julianna Margulies, a costar in his medical drama. "You can see them get weak at the knees." The waggish leading man of *Three Kings, O Brother, Where Art Thou?* and *Ocean's Eleven* is the son of a local TV host and nephew of singing legend Rosemary Clooney. "We always thought he would be a stand-up comic, he was so hilariously funny," said his dad, Nick, who put him on his Cincinnati variety show at 5. Instead, boy George headed into a decade of lesser TV roles before *ER.* After a three-year marriage to actress Talia Balsam ended in 1992, Clooney has lived in what he calls Casa de Clooney, an eight-bedroom bachelor pad in the Hollywood Hills, and has been linked with a revolving door full of ladies. This winter, he makes his feature film directorial debut with *Confessions of a Dangerous Mind,* about TV game-show host Chuck Barris. Why the switch to the other side of the camera? "There will be a period of time in the not-too-distant future when people will be sick of seeing you," he has said, half facetiously. "I'm sick of me already."

OBS

# mel gibson

## born January 3, 1956

What is that old Mel magic he weaves so well? Easy. He is just slightly, deliberately, brilliantly out of kilter. Consider the roles that kept bringing us back for more: the crazed moralist Mad Max; an around-the-bend Hamlet; the hair-triggered Martin Riggs in the four-part *Lethal Weapon* series and, not least, blue-faced William Wallace in *Braveheart*, which brought Gibson both Best Director and Best Picture Oscars. "A big part of his appeal comes from his personality," said his sometime outfitter Giorgio Armani. "After all, Mel is a character, something that comes through in the constant twinkle in his eye." Since those mischievous pool-blue eyes—and the sight of his bare behind—made him an international sex symbol in *Gallipoli* in 1981, Gibson has built a rep in the industry as a practical gagster (notoriously planting whoopee cushions and stink bombs on sets) and role-model family man. Transplanted by his folks from Upstate New York to Australia in 1968, Gibson calls an 800-acre ranch there home with Robyn, his wife of 22 years, and their seven kids. They now have also acquired properties stateside in California, Montana and Connecticut. Career-wise, he is shifting more into directing. "I think time makes one aware of the light and shade in human behavior," he has said, adding, "Most people get better with time. The sad part is, you get old and ugly as you get better." Right, Mel.

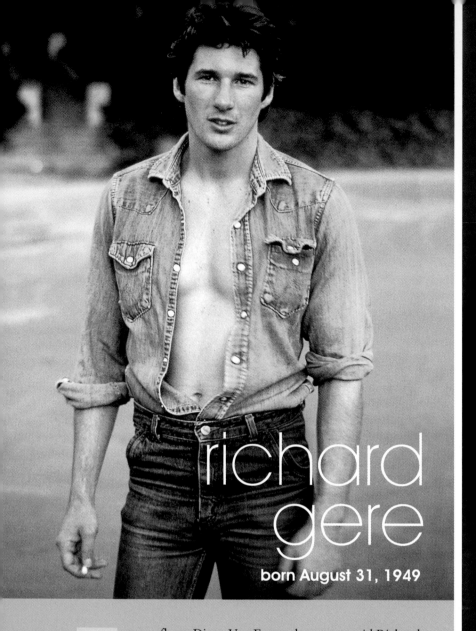

# richard gere

**born August 31, 1949**

Former flame Diane Von Furstenberg once said Richard Gere had struggled early because "he was the person who was *not* John Travolta." But the farm-raised pouty-lipped heartbreaker managed to put his own brand on Travolta's reject properties—*Days of Heaven, American Gigolo* and *An Officer and a Gentleman*. (That full-frontal scene in *Gigolo* didn't hurt.) "I thought he was the sexiest man alive," said *Heaven* costar Brooke Adams. What put him over the top was playing the jillionaire john who hired Julia Roberts in *Pretty Woman*. Reuniting with her in 1999's *Runaway Bride* established his sexy-forever status. He has kept the home fires stoked too. After a brief marriage to Cindy Crawford, he met *Law & Order*'s Carey Lowell, 41, with whom he has a son, 2½. The boy's middle name, Jigme ("fearless" in Tibetan), honors Gere's Buddhist faith. "His Holiness [the Dalai Lama] generates love and compassion to every human being," Gere has said. "I haven't made that leap yet. I haven't given up self-aspiration. I still like making movies."

Madonna famously failed to seduce him at a party shown in her 1991 documentary *Truth or Dare*. But Antonio Banderas is ever grateful for her audacity and the visibility. "Until then," he said, "I was known in America only as Pedro Almodóvar's actor by people who went to foreign films." The sexy Spaniard finally conquered Hollywood in 1992's *The Mambo Kings*—without speaking English (a coach taught him the script phonetically). "His intelligence—combined with his appearance—is the most seductive thing about him," said *Mambo* director Arne Glimcher. Within a year Banderas had mastered the language and mopped up as Tom Hanks's lover in *Philadelphia* and as a blood-sucking Parisian in *Interview with the Vampire*. Next he proved he could carry a movie in *Desperado* and make music with Madonna in *Evita*. In 1995 Melanie Griffith succeeded where the Material Girl had failed; Banderas split from his wife of nine years, actress Ana Leza, creating a tabloid firestorm. After painful divorces (Griffith's from Don Johnson), they wed in 1996 and had a daughter, Stella, now 5. Said Banderas: "You cannot go against love."

antonio
banderas

born August 10, 1960

# josh hartnett

**born July 21, 1978**

When he walks into a room, you know he's there," said *Pearl Harbor* producer Jerry Bruckheimer. "The camera just loves him," added *O* director Tim Blake Nelson. "He is extraordinarily charismatic." But credit ad stylist Rachel Zoe Rosenzweig for spotting what she saw as "the next Hollywood hottie" and launching him in a 1997 Tommy Hilfiger campaign. Since then, Josh Hartnett has had similar seismic impact in moving pictures—everything from teen horror fare (*Halloween: H₂O, The Faculty*) and indies (*The Virgin Suicides, O*) to the big-buzz circuit of *Pearl Harbor*. His *Harbor* costar Ben Affleck predicted that Hartnett would have "beautiful women camped out on his front lawn," but the industry's new hunk-and-a-half stood by his high school sweetheart, actress Ellen Fenster. Besides, his lawn is nearly 2,000 miles from L.A., in his native Minnesota, where he can more easily "fly under the radar." Fame, he has said, "is not something I seek." Funny, it (or is it she?) sure has drawn a bead on him.

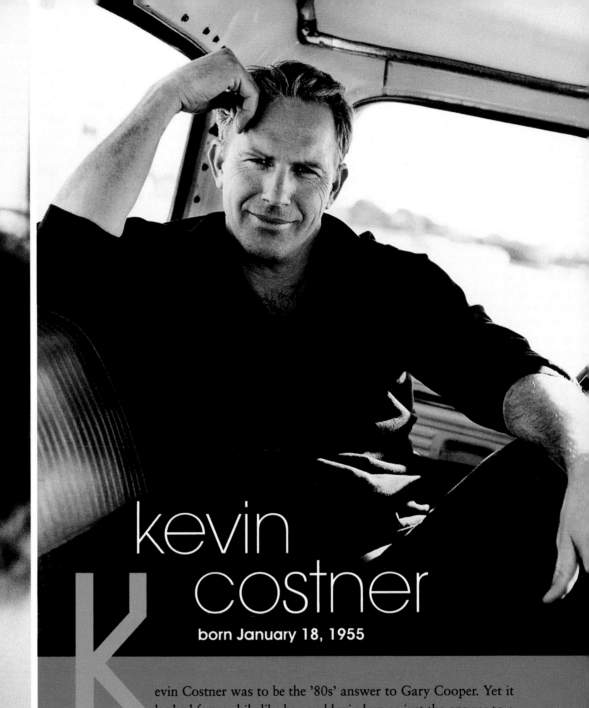

# kevin costner

born January 18, 1955

Kevin Costner was to be the '80s' answer to Gary Cooper. Yet it looked for a while like he would wind up as just the answer to a trivia question when his scenes in *The Big Chill* were cut (he was the dead guy). But soon his steamy romps with Sean Young in *No Way Out* and Susan Sarandon in *Bull Durham* set pulses—and ticket sales—racing, and studio mogul Mike Medavoy proclaimed him "one of the few international movie stars who have the old Hollywood glamor." Costner set himself on a nonstop schedule—16 movies in 12 years, including disappointments like *Waterworld* and *The Postman*. That frantic period also saw the end of his 16-year marriage to Cindy Silva (they have three kids). "He has nuclear energy," explained Mary McDonnell, his costar in the monument and vindication of his career, the 1990 Sioux epic *Dances with Wolves,* which he produced, directed and saw win seven Oscars, including Best Director and Best Picture. "I'm happy about the things I've done," said Costner. "Not always happy about the results but happy about the decisions, because I made them myself."

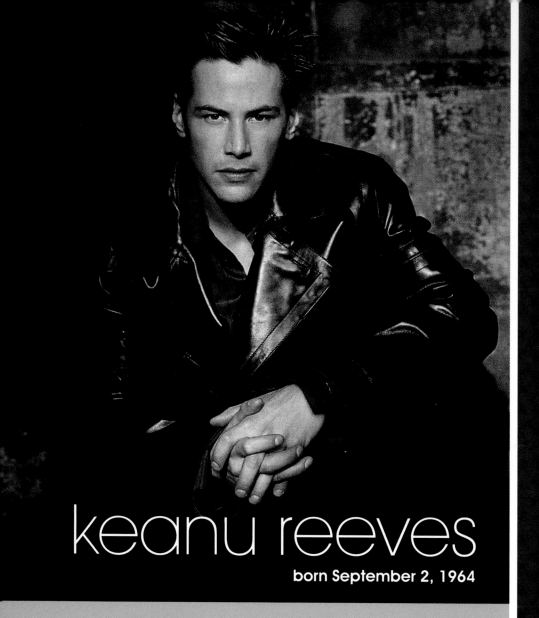

# keanu reeves
### born September 2, 1964

His slightly wooden style may be underappreciated by critics, but Keanu Reeves has carved himself one bitchin' career. After making his name as a dopey time-traveling dude in *Bill & Ted's Excellent Adventure,* he got cast by such discerning directors as Gus Van Sant (*My Own Private Idaho*) and Francis Ford Coppola (*Dracula*); Reeves even dropped his trademark expression—*whoa!*—to tackle a Shakespeare classic (*Much Ado About Nothing*). Then, with 1994's *Speed,* he vroomed into the fast lane. "What is nice about him as an action hero is that he's vulnerable on the screen," said the film's director, Jan De Bont. Keanu means "cool breeze over the mountains" in Hawaiian, and he has weathered some ill winds. He was left in infancy by his half-Hawaiian, half-Chinese dad, and in 1999 Reeves and girlfriend Jennifer Syme had a stillborn baby (Syme died last year in a car accident). Now filming two sequels to his megahit *The Matrix,* Reeves has long resided in an L.A. hotel between gigs with his rock band Dogstar and location shoots. "Acting is home for me," he has explained. "That is where I live."

While shooting *Titanic* in the chilly seas off Mexico, his leading man dithered and fussed before every immersion, director James Cameron later revealed. But come Christmas, 1997, Leonardo DiCaprio happily soaked it all up as Leomaniacs thronged like lemmings after Hollywood's latest big-scream idol. Though the *Titanic* tidal wave pushed his price nearly tenfold to $20 million per picture, the Los Angeles-born son of a hippie comic book artist and a legal secretary took a sabbatical, partying prodigiously with a string of supermodels, eventually settling in with Brazilian Gisele Bündchen. Quipped a Manhattan maître d': "Leo comes to clubs like you and I go to McDonalds." His eventual film follow-ups, *The Man in the Iron Mask* and *The Beach,* were relative disappointments, but the industry still believed in its quondam "king of the world." He had, after all, been nominated for an Oscar at 19 for *What's Eating Gilbert Grape* and possesses "enormous range," noted Baz Luhrmann, his director in *Romeo + Juliet.* Come hell or icy water, DiCaprio has kept it all in perspective. "You want to be remembered for your work," he observed, "rather than being sort of the hunk of the month."

leonardo
dicaprio

**born November 11, 1974**

# brad pitt

**born December 18, 1963**

"Next to that kid, we all look like onions," Dustin Hoffman said of his *Sleepers* costar. "Can you believe anybody's that good looking?" From the moment he sauntered into Geena Davis's motel room in 1991's *Thelma & Louise,* Brad Pitt has seduced audiences with looks so nice, PEOPLE chose to name him twice as its Sexiest Man Alive. But "apart from the fact that he's a gorgeous guy," said his *Legends of the Fall* costar Julia Ormond, "he's also someone who's constantly trying to shrug that off." To undercut his drool factor, which hit a new high in last year's *Ocean's Eleven,* the Oklahoma-born actor wore brown contacts over his baby blues for *12 Monkeys,* marred his stunning smile by sporting a chipped tooth for *Fight Club,* and grew a scruffy beard and disfigured his taut physique with tattoos for *Snatch.* "He doesn't want to feel trapped by people's expectations," director Terry Gilliam has said. "He knows there's more to him." After well-publicized disengagements from both Juliette Lewis and Gwyneth Paltrow, Pitt happily settled into a new role in 2000: husband. The woman who now—enviably—gazes daily upon his outer perfection and appreciates the inner humanity is of course Jennifer Aniston, 33, who shares a 20-room Hollywood Hills home with him (and their six dogs). "I feel like we're embarking on this journey together," exulted Pitt. "I've never done anything like it and have never experienced anything like it before in my life."

# MASTER CLA

## meryl streep

**born June 22, 1949**

S

he is, by overwhelming consensus, the most gifted actress of her time and shares, with Katharine Hepburn, the record for the most Oscar nominations (12). "If only she would giggle more and suffer less," the late critic Pauline Kael wrote, but in fact the New Jersey-bred Vassar grad was known as a clown and mimic at Yale Drama School, and has often ventured beyond the weepy gravitas of her heralded early roles. "She has wit, humor and passion," said Alan Pakula, director of *Sophie's Choice,* in which Streep played a Polish concentration camp prisoner forced to give up one of her children. But she proved equally adept as *Heartburn*'s cheated-on Washington wife or the jaded actress fighting addiction in *Postcards from the Edge.* In one of her most commercial roles, she donned yet another accent—Italian—as an Iowa-based war bride who discovers midlife passion with Clint Eastwood in *The Bridges of Madison County.* Grounded and private, Streep has found relief from the fame game in Connecticut with her sculptor husband of 23 years, Don Gummer, 55. A mother of four, she tried to work only during school vacations. Summing up her gift, Robert Benton, director of *Kramer vs. Kramer* (her first Oscar winner), noted that "she has an immense backbone of technique, but you never catch her using it." Of course not, Streep explained: "They don't want to see the geisha flossing, you know. They want to see her smile."

SS Here are the superpros of the silver screen, for whom acting is not a mere craft but an art

# russell crowe

**born April 7, 1964**

Russell Crowe took the lead of the so-called Aussie Posse of actors—and took home a 2000 Oscar—as the heroic Roman general of *Gladiator*. In conquering Hollywood, he wielded a pugnaciousness nearly as outsize as his talent. "He's highly intelligent, and he has this self-confidence that you could define as arrogance," confided Ron Howard, who directed Crowe's Oscar-nominated performance as the schizophrenic math genius in *A Beautiful Mind*. "I'm not arrogant. I'm focused," countered the New Zealand-born, Sydney-raised son of movie-set caterers. But bar brawls and public surliness didn't stop Sharon Stone from labeling him "the sexiest man working in movies" or from casting the then relative unknown as a reformed gunslinger in her 1995 production *The Quick and the Dead*. "He has grit and luminosity at the same time," she said. Those qualities also got the attention of Meg Ryan, whose brief fling with costar Crowe while filming 2000's *Proof of Life* helped end her marriage. Seeking relief, Crowe retreated to his farm north of Sydney and to 30 Odd Foot of Grunts, the rock band he fronted for 22 years and for which he wrote an early song entitled, tellingly, "I Want to Be Like Marlon Brando." In terms of buzz and controversy, he is well on his way, and with no damage to the bottom line. "At the end of it all," stressed *Gladiator* director Ridley Scott, "Russell's worth it. That's the key."

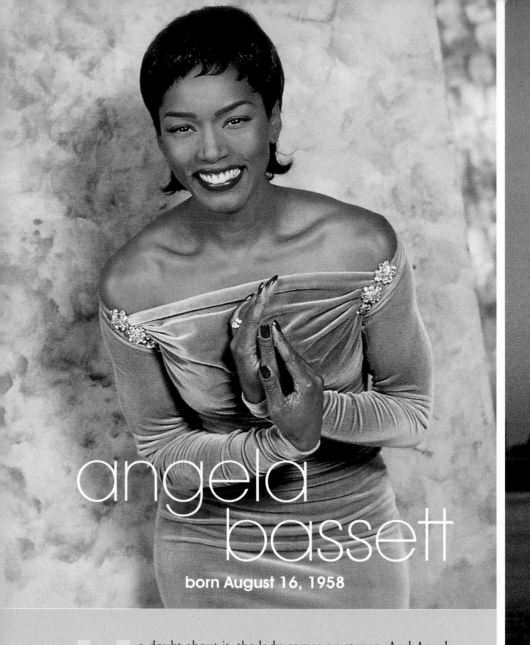

# angela bassett

**born August 16, 1958**

No doubt about it, the lady comes on strong. And Angela Bassett's force isn't just physical, despite the sinewy muscle she strutted as singer Tina Turner in 1993's *What's Love Got to Do With It?* She's equally handy with volcanic emotion, as when she set fire to her cheating husband's BMW in *Waiting to Exhale.* "I tend to stay in character the whole time I do a movie, and that's draining," admitted the Yale grad, raised in Florida by a struggling single mom. "I need to calm down." She did chill a bit in *How Stella Got Her Groove Back,* and producer Deborah Schindler found her "the embodiment of beauty and strength, and terrifically smart." Wes Craven, who directed Bassett in 1999's *Music of the Heart,* agreed: "It's her beauty and regal bearing—plus those abs and arms. It does something to your subconscious." Wed since 1997 to actor Courtney B. Vance, 42, Bassett is herself conscious of having found what Stella sought. "Being in a groove . . . is about being self-assured, confident," she said. "My life is joyful. I think that's pretty groovy."

Having attempted homicide in *A Perfect Murder,* philandered in *Fatal Attraction* and swindled in *Wall Street,* Michael Douglas is no Tom Hanks—though he did win an Oscar as Gordon Gekko in *Wall Street.* He "dares to play what could be considered non-user-friendly roles," suggested his *Falling Down* director Joel Schumacher. Working with the intensity of his famed father, Kirk, Douglas first delivered on the name as the producer of 1975's Best Picture, *One Flew Over the Cuckoo's Nest,* and remains unapologetic about such controversial choices as *Basic Instinct* and the sexual-harassment flick *Disclosure.* "Yes, you feel responsible for what you do," he argued, "but it's also my responsibility to make two hours of entertainment." Wed in 2000 to his *Traffic* costar Catherine Zeta-Jones, 32, Douglas may be mellowing now that his son Cameron, 23 (with ex-wife Diandra), has an infant half brother, Dylan. "I've just about run out of my repertoire of greedy, angst-ridden guys," he recently said. "And now I'm thinking it might be nice to make a movie that my new son can see."

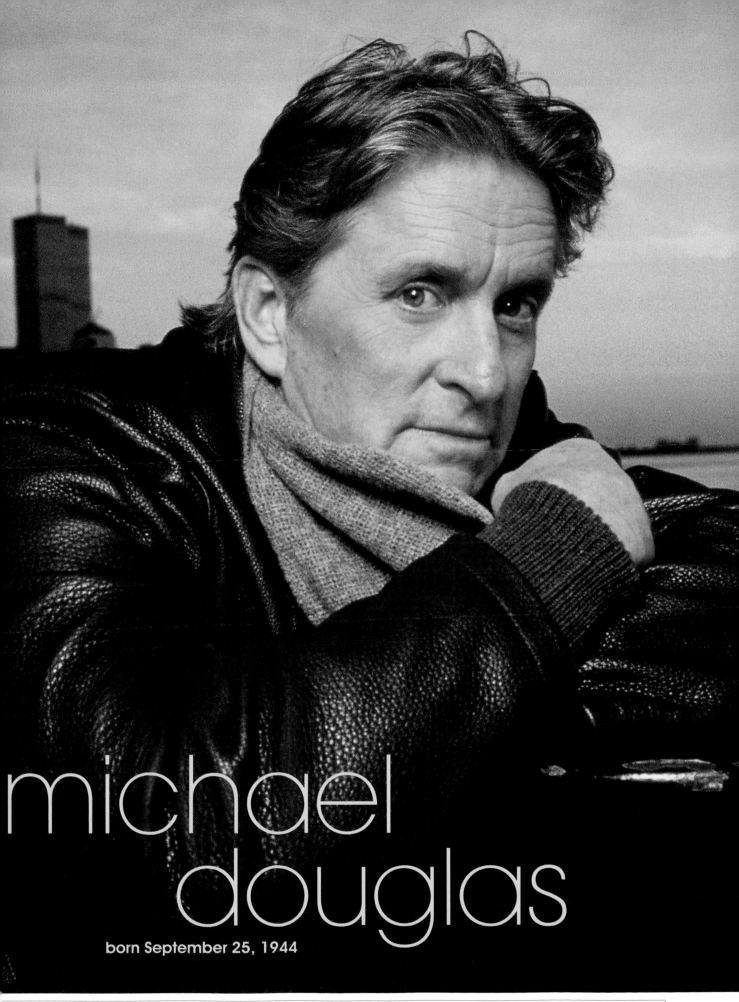

michael
douglas

**born September 25, 1944**

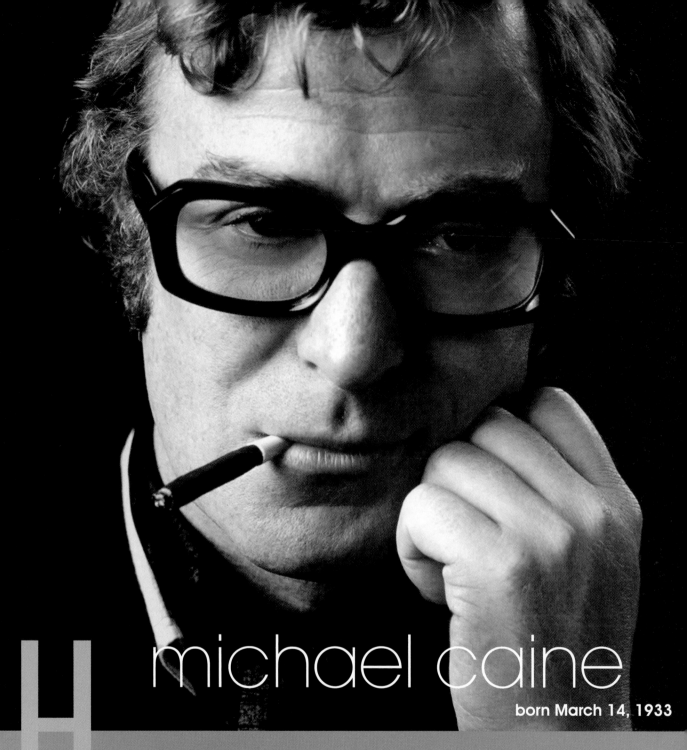

# michael caine

**born March 14, 1933**

H e came from the wrong side of the Thames, raised by a fish-market porter and a charwoman, and once toiled in a butter factory himself. But Maurice Micklewhite changed his name to Michael Caine and wound up showbiz royalty. After slipping on his trademark glasses to play a spy in *The Ipcress File* in 1965, Caine has starred in more than 80 films and got five Oscar nominations, starting with 1966's *Alfie* and capped by two Supporting Actor victories (*Hannah and Her Sisters* and *The Cider House Rules*). "I've done it all," he said. "I've been a gay, a killer, a lunatic, an adulterer, a seducer. A good time was had by all." As pal Roger Moore summed it up, "He's brave. He will tackle anything." He has been married 29 years to Shakira, 55, an ex-Miss Guyana. She's the mom of Natasha, 28. (Caine also has a daughter, Dominique, 46, from a first marriage.) The South London boy has now relocated to bucolic Surrey, but not to retire. "I cannot think of anything more frustrating," he said, "than to be sitting on a rocking chair on a porch at the end of your life, regretting the things that you didn't do."

In films like *White Palace* and *Bull Durham*, Susan Sarandon seduced the pants off her co-stars and audiences alike. But it took stripping herself of all glamor to play a dowdy, determined nun in *Dead Man Walking* to finally win an Oscar. (She had four previous nominations, including one for *Thelma & Louise*.) "It's too bad women are made to choose between being serious and sensual people," she said, but Sarandon has proven one can be both. She's a UNICEF ambassador and an outspoken activist who, with partner Tim Robbins, 43, disrupted the 1993 Oscars by prefacing her presenter remarks with a protest of the treatment of HIV-infected Haitian refugees. Divorced from actor Chris Sarandon in 1979, Sarandon has a daughter, Eva, 17 (whose dad is director Franco Amurri), and two sons, Jack, 13, and Miles, 10, with Robbins. The siren roles have decreased of late for the self-described "designated hitter for older ovaries." But "she's a sensual being," confirmed Dustin Hoffman, who plays her husband in this fall's *Moonlight Mile*. "And she will be for the rest of her life."

# susan sarandon

**born October 4, 1946**

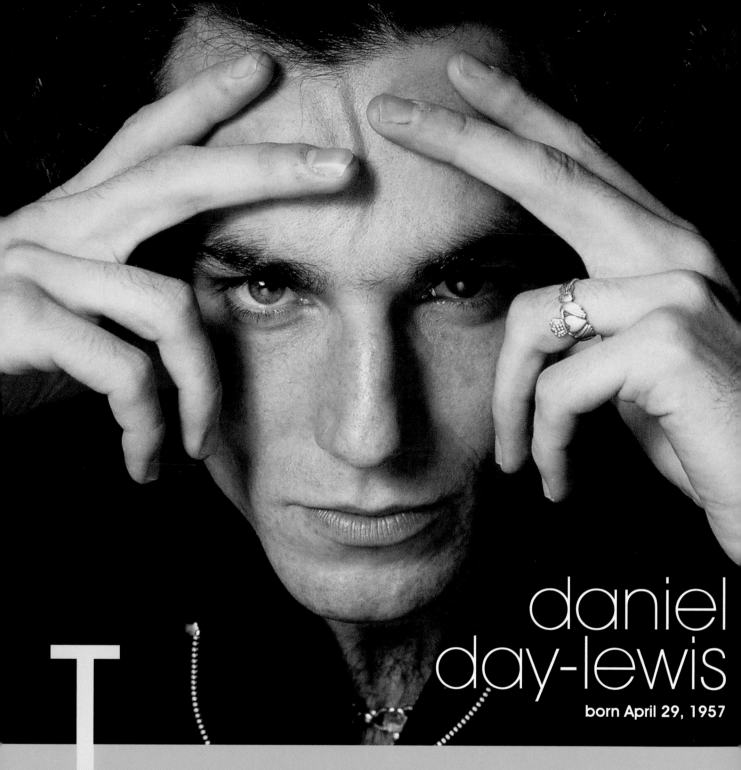

# daniel day-lewis

**born April 29, 1957**

**T**his thinking woman's sex symbol maintains he could happily not be a movie star. But what a waste if Daniel Day-Lewis had, as planned, wound up a furniture maker. Fortunately, the brooding son of a British poet laureate also trained at the Bristol Old Vic Theatre School and wound up winning an Oscar as the quadriplegic artist in 1989's *My Left Foot.* "He's fearless," said Michael Mann, who directed him in *The Last of the Mohicans.* "He will do and try anything." Known for immersing himself in roles, Day-Lewis was "engaging," reported Michelle Pfeiffer, his costar in *The Age of Innocence,* "but he really does keep things to himself." Not least his private life, which included liaisons with Julia Roberts and Juliette Binoche; Isabelle Adjani had his son in 1995. The following year he wed Rebecca Miller, 39, daughter of playwright Arthur Miller, and had another son. Finicky about roles, Day-Lewis took a four-year break before filming Martin Scorsese's *Gangs of New York.* "I can only be true to the impulses I have," he explained. "And those impulses come rarely."

As explosive New York narc Popeye Doyle in his 1972 Oscar winner *The French Connection*, Gene Hackman did some of his own driving during the frightening car chases and was later labeled by *Variety* "the hardest-working thesp in showbiz." Yet to this day the ex-Marine is uncomfortable with stardom and hasn't seen most of the nearly 80 features in which he has appeared. A pity, considering the gems in his oeuvre: tragicomic Buck Barrow in *Bonnie and Clyde*, the fascist sheriff in *Unforgiven* (for which he won a supporting Oscar) and the rogue patriarch of *The Royal Tenenbaums*, to name a few. Though renowned for his capacity to straddle violence and comedy, Hackman has described himself as "not a tough guy at all," just drawn to roles "with some emotional sting." The father of three (from his marriage to Faye Maltese) actually lives a gentle life in Santa Fe, writing fiction, painting and scuba diving with Betsy Arakawa, his second wife of 11 years. But mostly he acts—at a prolific pace. "I have that old thing in me from the early days when you couldn't get a job," Hackman once said. "You want to take everything that's offered."

# gene hackman

born January 30, 1930

**J**ohn Travolta's chanting "Al Pacino! Al Pacino!" to his mirror in *Saturday Night Fever* made it official: The Pacino mystique ruled the '70s. Whether he played a heroic cop (*Serpico*), botched a bank robbery (*Dog Day Afternoon*) or whacked his own brother (*The Godfather II*), the sad-eyed South Bronx kid could sway an audience—no matter how evil his character. "He has a two-hour face," said actor pal Chazz Palminteri. "You could see him on every frame for two hours in a movie and still love him." No wonder director Francis Ford Coppola fought Paramount to cast him as Michael Corleone, the linchpin of his eight-hour-plus *Godfather* trilogy—and one of the landmark characters of American cinema. Notoriously private and never wed, Pacino has romanced Diane Keaton, had a daughter, Julie, 12, with acting teacher Jan Tarrant, and in January 2001 became father of twins with current love Beverly D'Angelo. Along the way he has been honored with eight Oscar nominations and one win (for *Scent of a Woman*) but never made peace with fame. "I hope the perception is that I'm an actor," he said. "I never intended to be a movie star."

# al pacino
born April 25, 1940

**W**ith more than a dozen movies and an Oscar (for 1998's exuberant *Shakespeare in Love*) already under her teensy belt, Gwyneth Paltrow is one of Young Hollywood's busiest—and most respected—actresses. Not to mention most scrutinized for her romances with costars Brad Pitt (*Seven*), Ben Affleck (*Shakespeare, Bounce*) and Luke Wilson (*The Royal Tenenbaums*). "She's strong," discovered Steve Kloves, her *Flesh and Bone* director. "If you cast her, you're really making a choice. There's nothing generic about Gwynnie." Or, she has pointed out, nothing snooty despite her private-school rearing as daughter of actress Blythe Danner and director-producer Bruce Paltrow. "People have no real understanding of who I am," she declared. "If you sit up straight, chew with your mouth closed and have good manners, you're a snob." With last year's *Shallow Hal,* for which she donned a prosthetic "fat suit," moviegoers learned what Paul Thomas Anderson found directing her in 1996's *Hard Eight.* "Gwyneth isn't afraid to do anything," he said. "She is totally not afraid to be unglamorous or despicable or sad or funny or stupid." In other words, Paltrow is a director's dream.

# gwyneth paltrow

born September 27, 1972

# ROLE PLAYER

What a cornucopia of characters! Inside these troupers lies a whole multiplex of possibilities

# dustin hoffman

**born August 8, 1937**

Some actors disappear into their roles, but Dustin Hoffman goes further. Having donned bras, girdles and heels for 1982's *Tootsie,* "Dustin went out to restaurants as Dorothy Michaels, to test it," recalled the film's director, Sydney Pollack. Such painstaking research was de rigueur for the L.A.-born Hoffman ever since his breakthrough as *The Graduate*'s angst-ridden Benjamin Braddock in 1967. Over the next three decades, playing everything from a Times Square hustler (*Midnight Cowboy*) and crusading reporter (*All the President's Men*) to cartoonish pirate (*Hook*), he was sometimes branded "difficult." "He can't distinguish between a pimple and a tumor," said Arthur Penn, his director in *Little Big Man.* "Everything involves his total attention." Hoffman makes no apologies. "If I beg for another take and then another," he once explained, "it's usually because I think I can do it better." It's hard to argue with seven Oscar nominations—and victories for *Kramer vs. Kramer* and *Rain Man.* He and his wife, Lisa, 47, with whom he has four kids, now live in Los Angeles. He has two grown children from his first marriage, and an industry full of admirers. "I grew up watching and idolizing Dustin Hoffman," said *Rain Man* costar Tom Cruise. "He showed me how a great actor thinks."

glenn
close

born March 19, 1947

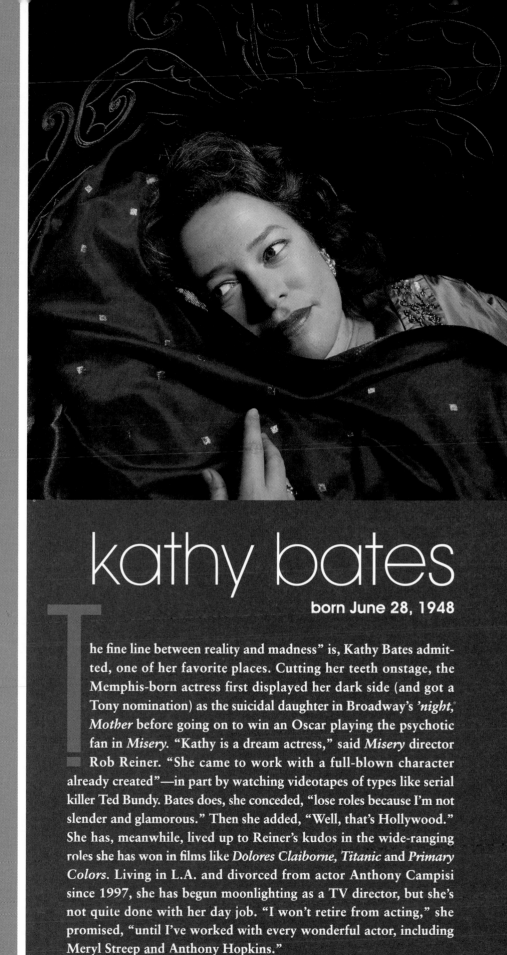

She horrified bunny lovers—and men—everywhere as Michael Douglas's spurned psychotic lover in *Fatal Attraction,* but Glenn Close had to fight for that career-changing role. After three consecutive Oscar nominations (*The World According to Garp, The Big Chill, The Natural*), the Connecticut-born actress found herself typecast as the Earth Mother of the '80s: solid as a rock and just about as exciting. "The question about me," she admitted, "was 'Can she be sexy?' " *Attraction* director Adrian Lyne bet yes and was rewarded, he found, when "an extraordinary erotic transformation took place. She was this tragic, bewildering mix of sexuality and rage!" That earned her yet another Oscar nod, and *Dangerous Liaisons* made it five. Close has also kept busy on stage and TV, with three Tony awards and an Emmy to show for it. Twice divorced, she and 14-year-old daughter Annie (with producer John Starke) reside quietly in a New York City suburb. "I know that I want to live my life simply," she once said, "so I can go out and do crazy and daring things in my work."

# kathy bates

### born June 28, 1948

The fine line between reality and madness" is, Kathy Bates admitted, one of her favorite places. Cutting her teeth onstage, the Memphis-born actress first displayed her dark side (and got a Tony nomination) as the suicidal daughter in Broadway's *'night, Mother* before going on to win an Oscar playing the psychotic fan in *Misery.* "Kathy is a dream actress," said *Misery* director Rob Reiner. "She came to work with a full-blown character already created"—in part by watching videotapes of types like serial killer Ted Bundy. Bates does, she conceded, "lose roles because I'm not slender and glamorous." Then she added, "Well, that's Hollywood." She has, meanwhile, lived up to Reiner's kudos in the wide-ranging roles she has won in films like *Dolores Claiborne, Titanic* and *Primary Colors.* Living in L.A. and divorced from actor Anthony Campisi since 1997, she has begun moonlighting as a TV director, but she's not quite done with her day job. "I won't retire from acting," she promised, "until I've worked with every wonderful actor, including Meryl Streep and Anthony Hopkins."

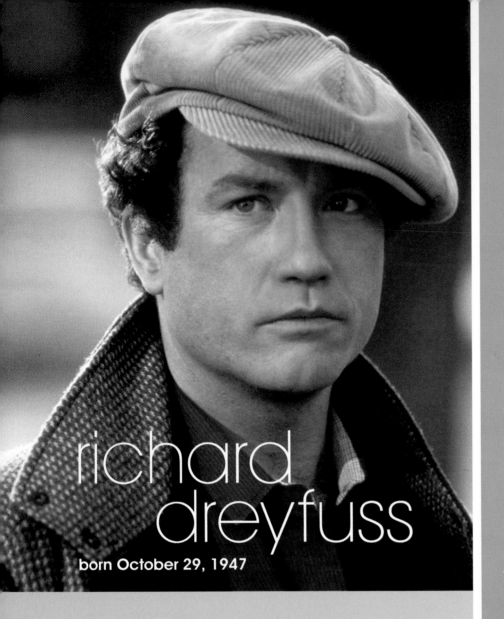

# richard
# dreyfuss

**born October 29, 1947**

Of his big-screen debut, in 1967's *Valley of the Dolls,* Richard Dreyfuss declared, "I am in the last 40 seconds of the worst film ever made." But shortly the cocky New York native (raised in California) was starring in some of the best, including *American Graffiti, Jaws* and *Close Encounters of the Third Kind.* "I definitely believed I was a talented guy," said the youngest ever recipient (at 30) of a Best Actor Oscar, for 1977's *The Goodbye Girl.* "His tendency is to do something to death or not at all," said Carrie Fisher of her pal, who ended years of alcohol and cocaine abuse with a horrific 1982 car wreck and arrest for drug possession. Sober, he copped an Oscar nod as a music teacher in 1995's *Mr. Holland's Opus.* Then the divorced father of three wed Janelle Lacey, 37, and took on series TV—as a cranky professor in *The Education of Max Bickford.* "I wanted to play a man of my age who's uncertain about his whole life, who's having a midlife crisis, who's not sure how to deal with women, work, sex, money," Dreyfuss explained. "I wanted to play me."

Graced with what Diane Sawyer called "one of those faces born to make us laugh and care," Michael J. Fox emerged in the '80s as Hollywood's best-loved Canadian. But at the height of the tsunami set off by his hit sitcom *Family Ties* and the *Back to the Future* trilogy, he asked himself, "Why me?" He switched from the sharp-witted nice-guy roles to darker films like *Casualties of War* but soon conceded, "I'm not a chameleon actor. I'm happy when people look at me in a movie and say, 'Well, we know him.'" In 1991 the actor suffered a personal setback. Diagnosed with Parkinson's, he anesthetized himself with alcohol until his wife, actress Tracy Pollan, and friends intervened. He returned to TV's less grueling schedule on *Spin City* in 1996, winning a fourth Emmy before leaving the show in 2000 to battle the disease through his own foundation. Living with Pollan, 42, and their four kids in New York City, Fox has lent his voice to *Stuart Little,* among other works, and plans to stay active producing, directing and writing. The title of his recent memoir says it all: *Lucky Man.*

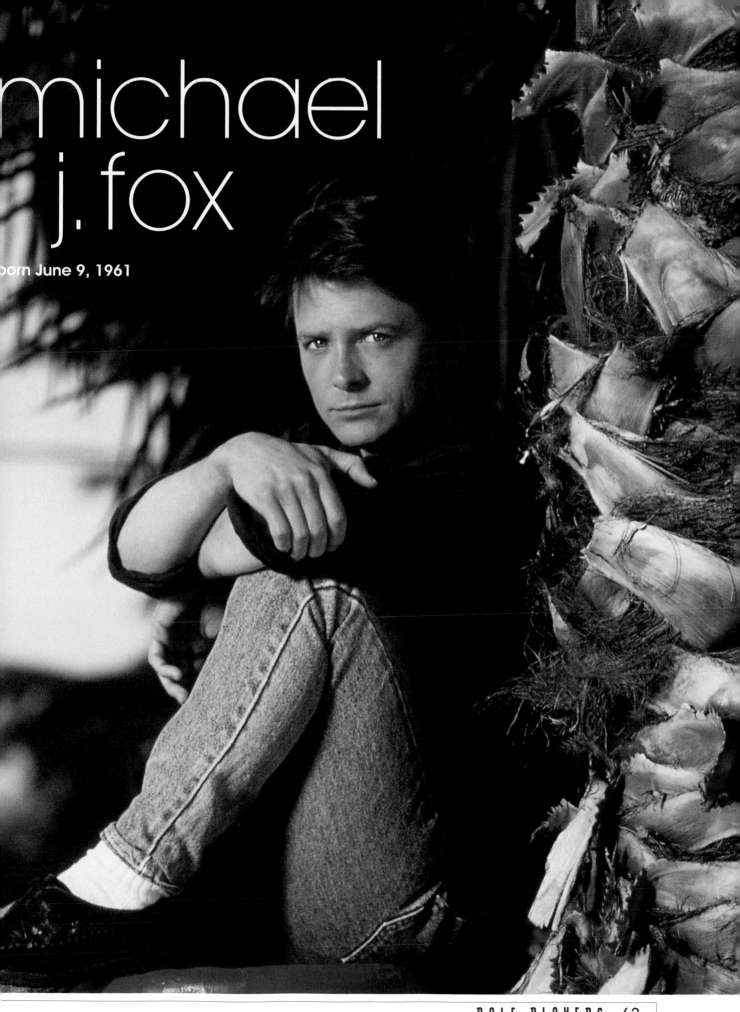

# michael j. fox

born June 9, 1961

# anjelica huston

**born July 8, 1951**

As a third-generation Oscar honoree (her father, John, won for directing *Treasure of the Sierra Madre*, and her grandfather Walter for acting in the 1948 classic), Anjelica Huston belongs to one of film's great dynasties. While growing up in Ireland, she recalls inscribing the words "I want to be an actress" into a baby book given to her by her ballerina mother, Enrica Soma (who died in a car accident when Huston was 17). In 1985 her father directed her to her Oscar win in *Prizzi's Honor*. He died in 1987, and two years later Huston ended a tumultuous 17-year relationship with *Prizzi's* costar Jack Nicholson. "Anjelica has a great vulnerability," observed her *Crimes and Misdemeanors* castmate Martin Landau. "She's had her share of pain, and she's able to tap into that." Married to sculptor Robert Graham since 1992, she has lightened up in recent years, playing the matriarch in *The Addams Family* and *The Royal Tenenbaums*. "When everything is so good," she said, "I'm apt to wonder what's coming that isn't so good. But all in all, I'm glad I'm out from under the dark clouds."

He made his first splash into acting at 8 in his dad's hit TV series *Sea Hunt*. Since then Lloyd Bridges' son Jeff has ridden an almost unbroken wave of critical praise, disappearing behind his leading-man looks into roles varying from the Texas football hero of *The Last Picture Show* (1971) to a shrewdly idealistic U.S. President in 2000's *The Contender*. (He joined brother Beau, 60, to play cocktail-lounge musicians in the 1989 charmer *The Fabulous Baker Boys*.) Though invariably genial and laid-back, "there are still waters that run very deep in him," said Mercedes Ruehl of her costar in 1991's *The Fisher King*. An avid musician and composer of more than 200 songs, Bridges has been married for 25 years to Susan Geston, 49, a photographer and the mother of their three daughters. Having yet to nab an Academy Award despite four nominations, he was pronounced by *The New York Times* the screen's "most underappreciated great actor of his generation." "But I feel appreciated," Bridges begged to differ. "I'm having a great career. I'm getting paid a lot of money. I'm getting a variety of roles. I'm doing what I want to do. What's the problem?"

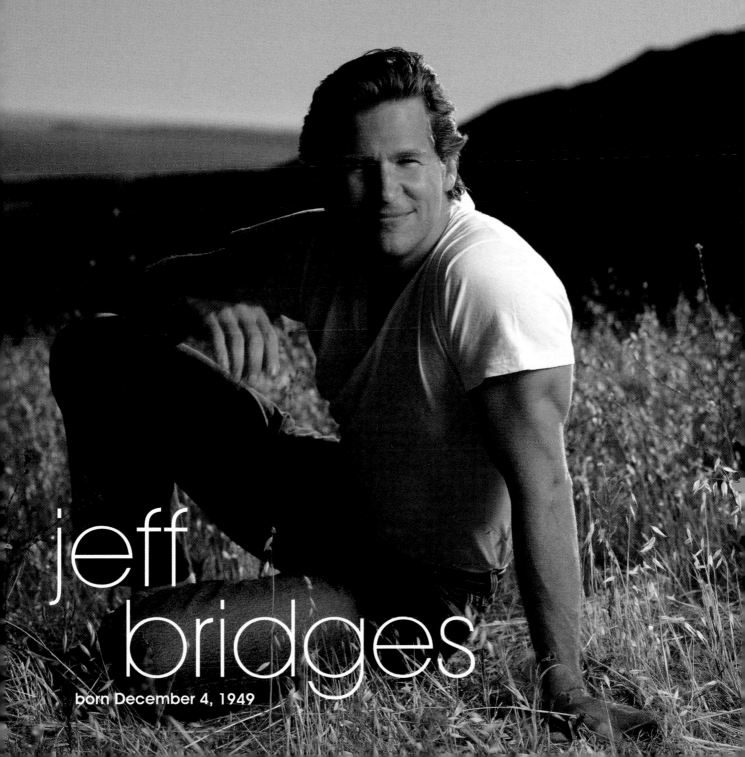

# jeff bridges

born December 4, 1949

# kevin spacey

born July 26, 1959

His face is so utterly nondescript it wouldn't stand out in a lineup of accountants, but Kevin Spacey "is capable of making the hair stand up on the back of your neck," observed Sam Mendes, who directed his seething Oscar-winning portrayal of a doomed suburbanite in *American Beauty.* That superficial blandness makes the New Jersey-born Juilliard dropout sublimely believable, and it didn't hurt that he apprenticed onstage in Chekhov and Shakespeare or that Jack Lemmon was his mentor. Spacey took his first Oscar as a fiendish felon in 1995's *The Usual Suspects.* "People assume I'm as complex as the characters I play, and I'm not," noted the ace mimic (who made a brief stab at stand-up comedy after high school). A fiercely private bachelor, Spacey lives in Manhattan when he's not on location or returning to his second home, the theater. "What Kevin manages to do with his acting is hint at all these other layers— the darker aspects, the secrets, the disappointments, the ironic humor," said Howard Davies, who directed him in a 1999 Broadway revival of O'Neill's *The Iceman Cometh.* "And that hinting is very, very attractive."

As Louie De Palma, the dictatorial squirt who dispatched cabs and venom on the late-'70s sitcom *Taxi,* Danny DeVito created what *TV Guide* called the most popular television character ever. In the ensuing two decades, DeVito has perfected the slimeball we hate to love on the big screen as, variously, a murderous bumbler (*Throw Momma from the Train*), a sleazy conniver (*Get Shorty*) and a comic-book villain (the Penguin in *Batman Returns*). "For some reason everybody from screenwriters to producers to audiences loves the idea of the greedy little tyrant," he said, "and I give them Napoleon on steroids, so they love me." Originally a New Jersey hairdresser ("I once did 35 heads on a New Year's Eve!"), DeVito broke through in 1975's *One Flew Over the Cuckoo's Nest.* "Like all great actors, there's a sense of danger about Danny," said *Tin Men* costar Barbara Hershey. "A sense that anything could happen." He has branched into producing (*Pulp Fiction*) and directing (*Death to Smoochy*). Actress Rhea Perlman, 54, his wife of 20 years and mother of their three teens, confided that "he can be quite a taskmaster behind the camera, but when we get home, I give the directions."

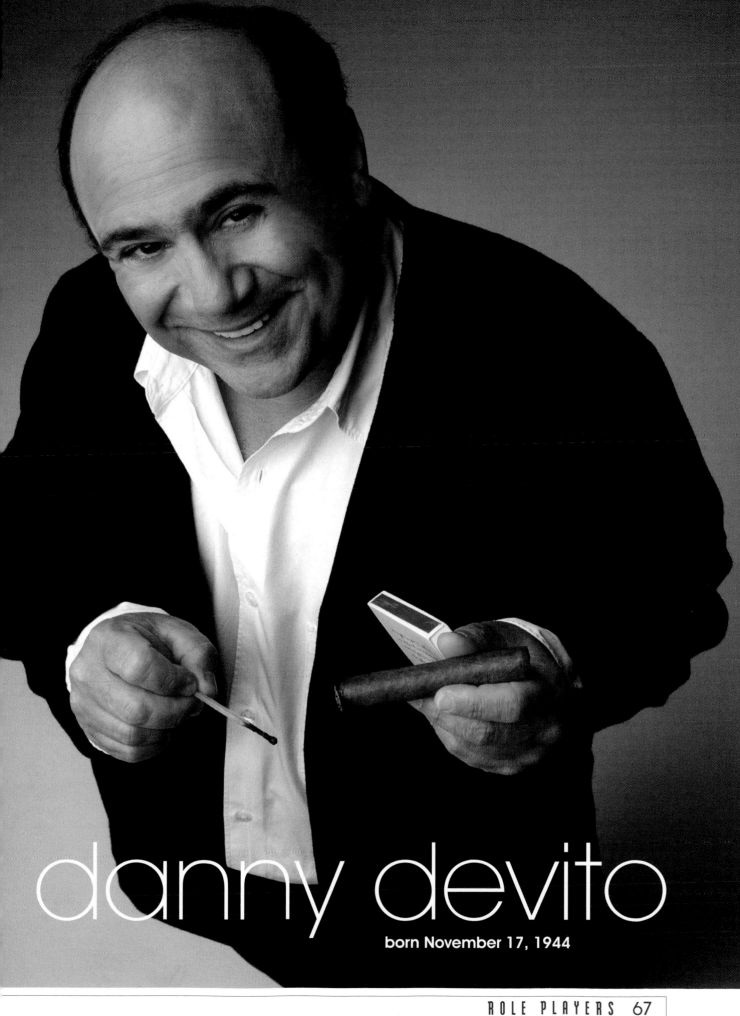

# danny devito

born November 17, 1944

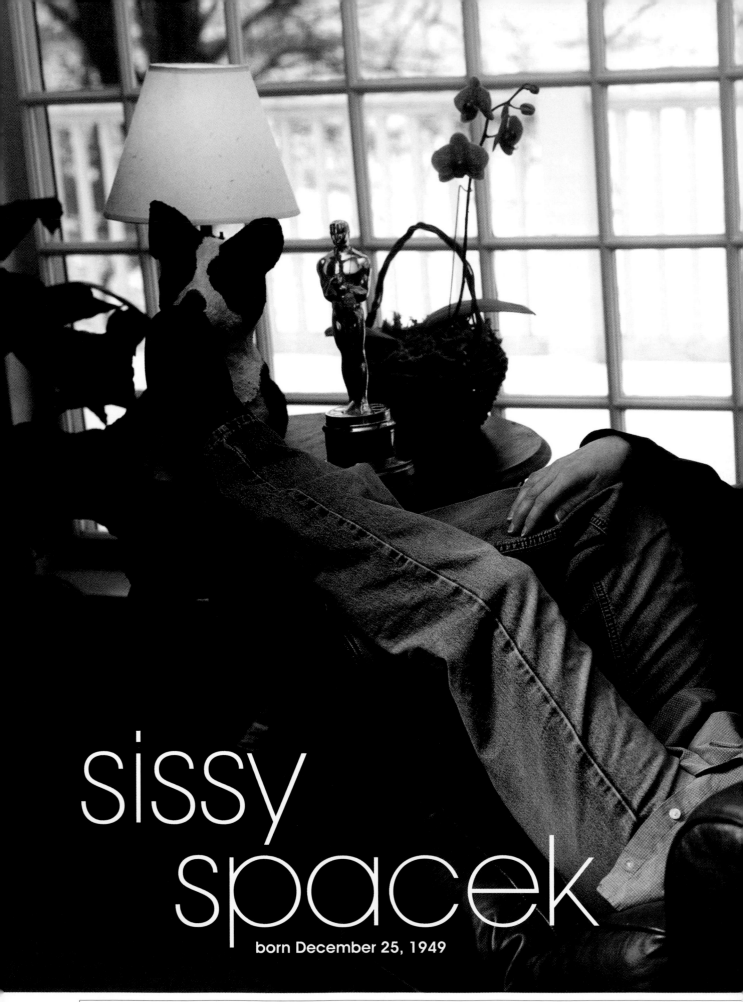

# sissy spacek

born December 25, 1949

A Texas-born tomboy nicknamed Sissy by her two older brothers, Mary Elizabeth Spacek shot to fame in 1976's horror hit *Carrie* as a high school outcast who wreaks telekinetic vengeance on her tormentors. Four years later, the freckle-faced cousin of actor Rip Torn walked off with an Oscar—for her dead-on portrayal of country queen Loretta Lynn in *Coal Miner's Daughter* (in which Spacek sang the vocals instead of lipsynching). "I was amazed with her spirit, how much alike she and Loretta were," said director Michael Apted. "Sissy was the real thing." Her knack for playing typical folk with exceptional fortitude became evident in *Missing, The River* and *Crimes of the Heart,* elevating Spacek to one of the preeminent stars of the '80s. But, as *Crimes* castmate Jessica Lange indicated, "Sissy's life was always more important than her career." So at the peak of her popularity, she and production-designer husband Jack Fisk, 56, left L.A. for a Virginia farm, where they raised two daughters, Schuyler, 20, and Madison, 13. "I found that motherhood dwarfed everything else," Spacek said. For two decades she worked intermittently and only when she felt a project had "redeeming social value." That included 2001's wrenching *In the Bedroom,* which stirred a renewed storm of adulation and garnered her a sixth Oscar nomination. "It's fantastic that this film broke through," said actress friend Amy Irving. "Sissy is the kind of person you root for."

DOUBLE

# THREATS

They not only acted up a storm but also did the old song and dance

## jennifer lopez

**born July 24, 1969**

ears before there was a Puff Daddy or a chauffeured Mercedes, before she wore see-through Chanel, back when she was just a Catholic schoolgirl up in the Bronx, Jennifer Lopez startled her dad by announcing that she was joining the track team. Computer technician David Lopez worried, "because she'd never done anything like that. I thought she'd get outclassed." Jennifer? No way. She wound up competing in Madison Square Garden's Colgate Games. The show world first discovered this "tough chick," as director Oliver Stone characterized her, as a "fly girl" dancer on TV's *In Living Color.* Then she broke through in pictures in 1997, playing slain Tejano singer Selena, and has since become a moonlight diva and Hollywood's highest-paid Latina actress ever—at $10 mil per film. When *The Wedding Planner* opened in 2001, she was the first entertainer to have the top-grossing movie and No. 1 non-soundtrack album in the same week. She split with Puffy Combs after his infamous 1999 nightclub shoot-out and in 2001 wed Cris Judd, 32, a dancer in her "Love Don't Cost a Thing" video. "I want everything," Lopez once declared. "I want family. I want to do good work. I want love." The smart money doesn't bet against J.Lo.

Wowing 'em at the 2001 American Music Awards.

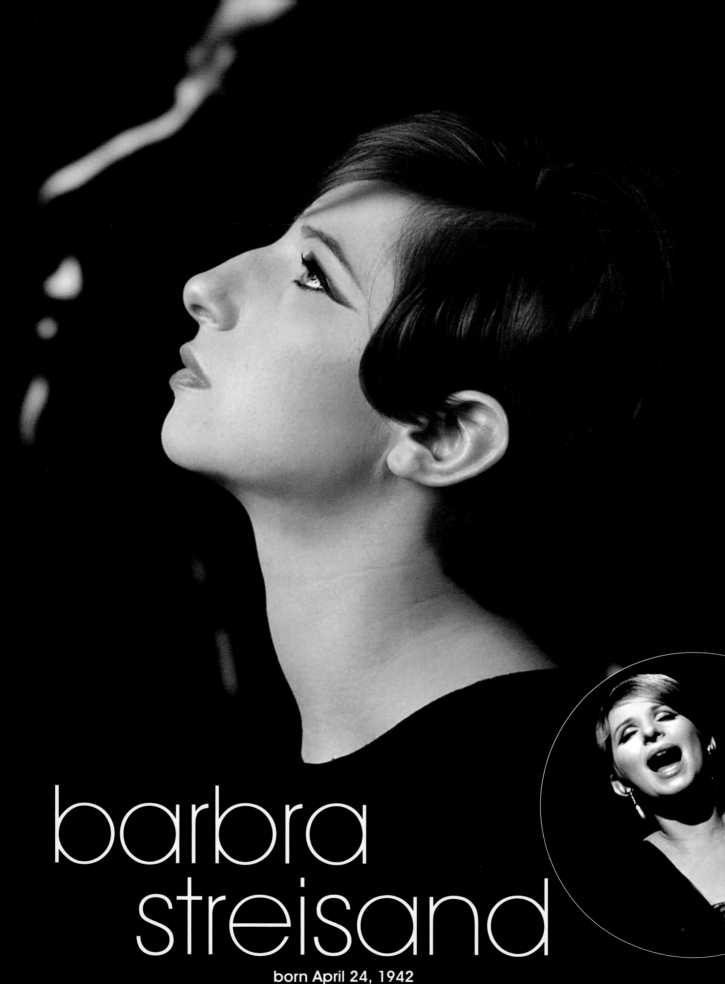

# barbra streisand

**born April 24, 1942**

**P**lacated for a "good" rehearsal of *Funny Girl*, the 1964 Broadway show that launched her boundary-breaking career, Barbra Streisand barked at producer Ray Stark: "I have to be great or nothing!" That standard has well served the Oscar-, Emmy- and Grammy-winning kid from Brooklyn with the admittedly imperfect beauty. She has done it all: acted (in films like *What's Up, Doc?* and *The Way We Were*), produced (*A Star Is Born, The Main Event*), wrote (*Yentl*) and directed (*The Prince of Tides*)—while recording dozens of smash albums and trying to be a player on the political scene.

Love seemed to take a backseat. She was married to Elliott Gould for eight years (actor son Jason is 35), then had romances with movie bigs like Ryan O'Neal and Jon Peters. In 2000, two years after marrying James Brolin, now 60, she embarked on a farewell concert tour, to have "more time to live life."

Belting one out in the 1968 film version of *Funny Girl.*

# liza minnelli
### born March 12, 1946

**I** never sang my mother's songs or used my father's name to get a job." So boasted the only daughter of the legendary Judy Garland and Oscar-winning director Vincente Minnelli (*Gigi*). Carving out "a lifetime of my own work," she released her first solo album at 18, collected a Tony at 19 and by 27 had won an Oscar for *Cabaret.* Her biggest box office success came in 1981's boozy comedy *Arthur.* "People would fall down laughing at Dudley Moore," recalled director Steve Gordon. "But they wanted to reach out and touch Liza. It's as if some bit of her magic would rub off on them." Clearly she inherited the cult following of her mom, who died of a drug overdose at 47. In recovery herself, Minnelli has had two hips replaced and, in 2000, a life-threatening bout of viral encephalitis. But in the words of *Cabaret* lyricist Fred Ebb, "If she couldn't entertain, she would just want to curl up and die." Thus, in 2002, Minnelli scheduled a European tour. Her performance of the year, however, was an all-star wedding spectacle with her fourth husband, producer David Gest. Elizabeth Taylor was a matron of honor, Michael Jackson the best man.

In the 1977 Broadway musical *The Act.*

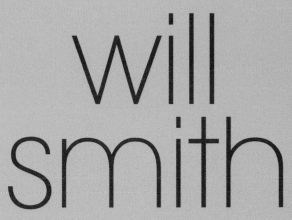

# will smith

**born September 25, 1968**

Behind the what's-not-to-love grin, Will Smith has it all figured out. First, that he is America's most beloved comic-action hero—not to mention pretty handy with a theme song. Second, that that's just a warm-up. "My goal," he has declared, "is to be the most diverse actor in the history of Hollywood." And if his Oscar nomination for *Ali,* the four Grammys and the $20 million paychecks were to disappear tomorrow, there's always plan B: "I absolutely believe I could be the President of the United States." Why not? Mr. Smith would not be the first actor to go to Washington, and his infectious braggadocio has already propelled him from high school math nerd in middle-class Philadelphia to latter half of the superstar rap duo DJ Jazzy Jeff and the Fresh Prince. "His self-confidence is so winning that you want him to teach you how to be like him," said Barry Sonnenfeld, who directed him in the 1997 blockbuster *Men in Black.* Smith himself spent two years learning to be like Muhammad Ali, gaining 35 lbs. and KO'ing any lingering doubt that he was an acting flyweight. "My drive and focus and my discipline are . . . darker than my image," noted the father of three, wed since 1997 to actress Jada Pinkett, 30. "I want to be the standard," he stated. "I want Tom Cruise to take movies that I turn down."

**Rapping when he was still Fresh.**

Almost 40 years have passed since Mary Poppins blew in on her magic umbrella, wooing the world with spoonfuls of sugar. With that Oscar-winning role, and her follow-up as the impetuous governess Maria in *The Sound of Music,* Julie Andrews deployed her proper British diction, cropped boyish coif and lilting voice to become the fantasy nanny of a generation—and a global treasure of song and screen. Director Blake Edwards, her husband since 1969, has said that even in a room full of children who don't know *Mary Poppins* or *The Sound of Music,* his wife is "like a magnet. They just go right to her." Over the decades, the offscreen mother of three also played against type, appearing topless in *S.O.B.* and bending gender in 1982's *Victor/Victoria.* But in most minds, she is forever our fair lady. Sadly, in 1997 her crystalline singing voice was silenced by botched throat surgery. But she soldiered on, appearing in *The Princess Diaries* and writing children's books. And, invoking that familiar Poppins pluck, she vowed: "Somehow, some way, I will sing again."

Onstage in 1980.

# julie
# andrews

**born October 1, 1935**

# bette midler

**born December 1, 1945**

I wanted to be a phenomenon, I didn't want to be a schlepper." With that credo, plus matching brassy hair and sassy outlook, Bette Midler left Honolulu for a career that has covered the waterfront. As the Divine Miss M, a bawdy chanteuse with cleavage to spare, she broke out of Manhattan's gay club scene to conquer Carnegie Hall in a mermaid costume. As vivid on film as onstage, she earned an Oscar nomination for her debut in 1979's *The Rose* and really hit her jaunty stride in '80s comedies (*Down and Out in Beverly Hills*) and 1996's *The First Wives Club*. Along the way, she also collected three Emmys, headlined a short-lived sitcom and emerged, said composer Marc Shaiman, as "one of the last real entertainers." Midler has settled with her husband, Martin von Haselberg, 53, a former performance artist, and teenage daughter Sophie in Manhattan. Schlepper-averse as ever, she has become a masterful player on the philanthropic scene, restoring public parks in the teeming city. "People always love a broad," she said of her life force. "Someone with a sense of humor, someone with a fairly wicked tongue, someone who can belt out a song and takes no guff."

**Headlining in concert with her favorite foils, the Harlettes.**

# cher

born May 20, 1946

Before *Silkwood* started shooting in 1982, cowriter Nora Ephron recalled frequent queries about the cast. When she would reply that Cher was playing opposite Meryl Streep (who had the title role of the whistleblower in a nuclear plant), folks would gasp, "You're kidding!" "We just told people, 'Trust us.'" Cher has a history of stirring doubt and dismay followed by vindication. She was nominated for an Oscar for *Silkwood* and then four years later took home a statuette for the romantic classic *Moonstruck*. In becoming the undisputed champ of rock and reel, not to mention the godmother of reinvention, Cher has also notched a Top 10 song every decade since 1965. "I've had so many rebirths," Cher (born Cherilyn Sarkisian in El Centro, California) has said, "I should come with my own midwife."

She roared into 2002, releasing a well-reviewed electrodance album, *Living Proof*, but has always believed that her true vocation was acting. She remembers being told "that's ridiculous," when she broached the idea to Sonny Bono, who flamboyantly piloted her liftoff on the club circuit and network TV before their divorce in 1975. "Some years I'm the coolest thing that's ever happened, and the next everyone's so over me," she has said. But she keeps turning back time, confounding us with her latest guy or plastic surgery. Her daughter by Bono, gay rights activist Chastity, is now 33; and her musician son Elijah Blue, by rocker second husband Gregg Allman, is 26. Cher "reminds me of a teenager," said *Mermaids* costar Winona Ryder. "She's got a young spirit." That, of course, is her credo. "Unless you risk looking foolish," she once said, "you never have the possibility of looking great."

In concert at Jones Beach in New York.

# john travolta

## born February 18, 1954

John Travolta owned the '70s. On TV's *Welcome Back, Kotter,* his Vinnie Barbarino made "Up your nose with a rubber hose" a cultural catchphrase. Then in *Saturday Night Fever,* he electrified the big screen with his dancing and landed an Oscar nomination. "He has the most energy I've ever encountered," marveled costar Karen Lynn Gorney. But the *Kotter* poster boy who ruled the disco floor and Hollywood with follow-ups like *Grease* and *Urban Cowboy* lost momentum in the '80s, as one flop followed another, including *SNF*'s sequel, *Staying Alive.* It was a dizzying rise and fall for the New Jersey-born high school dropout, the youngest of six children of a tire-shop owner and a drama coach. Finally, in 1994, he rebounded as a heroin addict/hit man in *Pulp Fiction,* turning in a funky twist with Uma Thurman for his second Oscar nod. To *Fiction* director Quentin Tarantino, he had reemerged as "one of the best stars Hollywood's ever produced." Hits like *Get Shorty* and *Face/Off* and $10-$20 million paydays confirmed he was back. A member of the controversial Church of Scientology, Travolta revels in a private life as high-flying as his career (he owns and pilots two planes). With his actress wife, Kelly Preston, 39, he has a son, Jett, 10, and a daughter, Ella Bleu, 2. And clearly, making time for family is important to a star whose most memorable pictures include a still of rocking the Reagan White House with the late Princess Diana.

Catching *Saturday Night Fever.*

Armed to the teeth with artifice and ammo, these gutsy guys—and gal (and their stuntmen)—left fans agasp

# sylvester stallone

**born July 6, 1946**

o, America. He came from nowhere to make his name—and nickname Sly—by cajoling skeptical studio heads into letting him star in a little script he'd banged out about a boxer from Philly, a lovable underdog who loses the big fight but wins the girl and his self-respect. Ten Oscar nominations and $117 million in ticket sales later, *Rocky* was named Best Picture of 1976. Over the years, the sleepy-eyed, mumble-mouthed Sylvester Stallone became a punching bag for critics but bulletproof at the box office. Action addicts swarmed to four *Rocky* sequels and cheered as the body count mounted toward the moon in his three-installment saga of an unstable ex-Green Beret named *Rambo.* He was more daring, artistically, in 1997, playing a sad-sack New Jersey lawman in *Cop Land* and holding his own with heavyweight thespians Robert De Niro and Harvey Keitel. That also seemed to be a watershed year personally, when he wed model Jennifer Flavin, now 33 and the mother of three of his five children. He had two earlier marriages, including a tempestuous quickie with Danish model Brigitte Nielsen. Stallone doesn't rule out a return to the ring as Rocky Balboa and makes no apologies for his macho, melodramatic body of work. "The Bible is action-packed," noted the Italian Stallion. "The Koran is action-packed. Even Buddha had a few moments of suspense in his life."

Oh, he's tough, all right—tough to categorize. Film's ultimate antihero—the cowboy killer of *The Good, the Bad and the Ugly* and the lean, mean vengeance machine known the world over as Dirty Harry—has evolved far beyond his stereotype as a gaunt, great-lookin' gunslinger. Similarly, the man of few but memorable words like "Go ahead, make my day" has expanded his flinty vocal range, now flipping off wry, cool one-liners in movies such as *True Crime* and *Space Cowboys*. In the process Clint Eastwood has become one of history's top-grossing stars and a magnum force on both sides of the camera. Beginning with 1971's jolting *Play Misty for Me*, he has also directed 22 films, including *Bird*, the lovely tribute of a piano-playing jazz fan to sax legend Charlie Parker. "Clint discovered his artistry as his audiences did, gradually, over time," noted Morgan Freeman, a costar in his antiviolence western *Unforgiven*. Eventually the Academy took notice, awarding that 1992 epic both Best Picture and Best Director Oscars. Three years later, no less than Meryl Streep called working on his calm, efficient *Bridges of Madison County* set "one of my favorite things I've ever done in my life." Off location, Eastwood hangs in Carmel, California, where he was once mayor, with his second wife, former TV newscaster Dina Ruiz, 36, and their daughter Morgan, 5. (Eastwood has six other kids.) Ever laconic, he pays no heed to being iconic. "It would be terrible to play me in person," he once said, dismissing a proposed bioflick. "I'd be boring as crap in a movie."

# clint eastwood

born May 31, 1930

# jackie chan

**born April 7, 1954**

Finally! It took Asian martial-arts star Jackie Chan some 16 years to crack the American market, and when he did—with 1996's *Rumble in the Bronx*—this kick-butt king cracked us up. "I love action but not violence," he explained. Chan Kwong-Sang (as he was born in Hong Kong) regards himself as a student of Buster Keaton rather than of chop-socky legend Bruce Lee, and he developed his mix of self-deprecating slapstick and balletic, thrill-inducing stunt-work in some 40 flicks before arriving stateside.

"Jackie's charming, down to earth, and he's a superstar," cheered Brett Ratner, who directed Chan and comedian Chris Tucker in the smash 1998 buddy film *Rush Hour* (and its monstrous-grossing 2001 sequel). To warn off would-be imitators, Chan ends his films with outtakes of stunts gone awry and the resulting multiple fractures. What won't he try? The now separated father of an 18-year-old son has decreed: "No sex scenes. No make love. The kids who like me don't need to see it. It would gross them out."

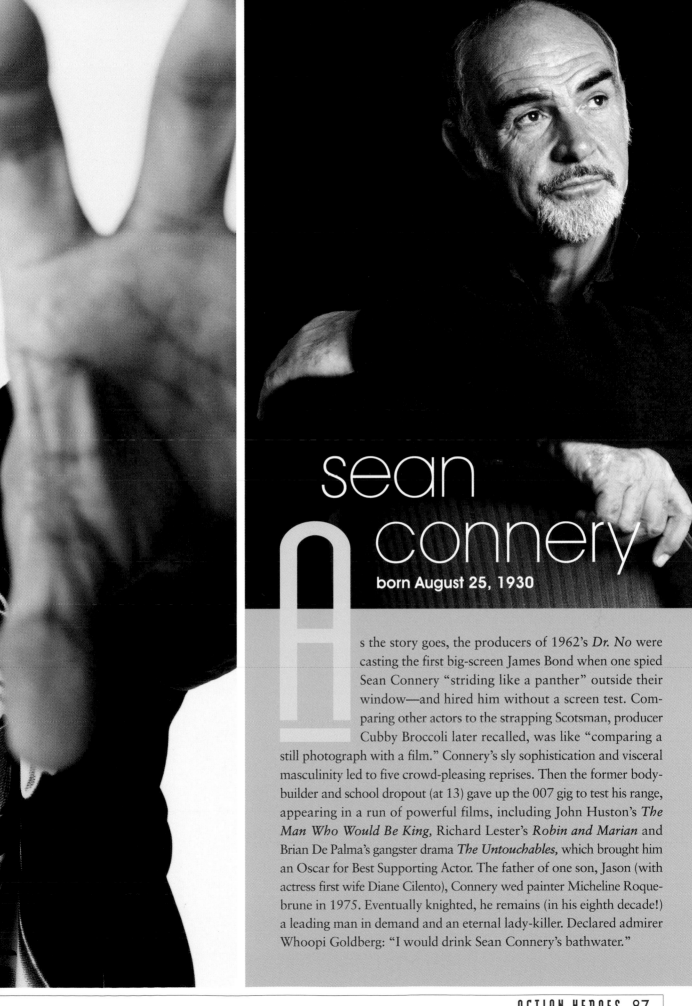

# sean connery

**born August 25, 1930**

As the story goes, the producers of 1962's *Dr. No* were casting the first big-screen James Bond when one spied Sean Connery "striding like a panther" outside their window—and hired him without a screen test. Comparing other actors to the strapping Scotsman, producer Cubby Broccoli later recalled, was like "comparing a still photograph with a film." Connery's sly sophistication and visceral masculinity led to five crowd-pleasing reprises. Then the former bodybuilder and school dropout (at 13) gave up the 007 gig to test his range, appearing in a run of powerful films, including John Huston's *The Man Who Would Be King*, Richard Lester's *Robin and Marian* and Brian De Palma's gangster drama *The Untouchables*, which brought him an Oscar for Best Supporting Actor. The father of one son, Jason (with actress first wife Diane Cilento), Connery wed painter Micheline Roquebrune in 1975. Eventually knighted, he remains (in his eighth decade!) a leading man in demand and an eternal lady-killer. Declared admirer Whoopi Goldberg: "I would drink Sean Connery's bathwater."

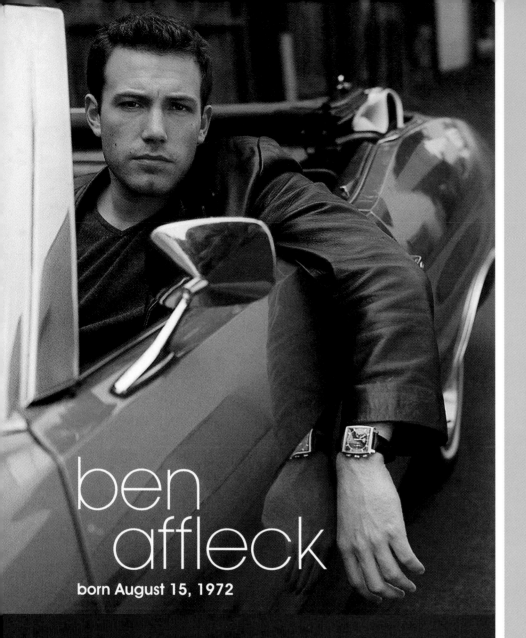

# ben affleck

## born August 15, 1972

He has been called swaggering and cocksure, but Ben Affleck claims to be "haunted by insecurity." He has leading-man looks, but he seldom gets the girl (*Pearl Harbor, Shakespeare in Love*). Yet he and school pal Matt Damon became Hollywood golden boys after sharing a Best Screenplay Oscar for 1997's *Good Will Hunting,* and something must have been in the water in Cambridge, Massachusetts, where he (and actor kid brother Casey) grew up with a schoolteacher mom and a blue-collar dad. "Women want to be with him and men want to be like him," said his *Armageddon* producer, Jerry Bruckheimer. That charm led to a romance with Gwyneth Paltrow and challenging choices, from indie films like *Dogma* to following Harrison Ford as CIA agent Jack Ryan in *The Sum of All Fears.* In between, in 2001 Affleck battled alcohol abuse in rehab, then returned to work, juggling producing and acting projects and eyeing another prize: "My fantasy is that someday I'm independently wealthy enough that I can run for Congress."

It started with an Emmy-winning smirk that charmed viewers of the late-'80s TV hit *Moonlighting.* Hollywood careers have been built on less, but beneath that look and his now signature stubble lay a wiseacre wit and a good-guy/bad-boy machismo destined to make marquee magic on the multiplex circuit. With the *Die Hard* trilogy, the welder's son from suburban New Jersey suddenly found himself in the $20-million-a-movie club. Similar sagas like *Armageddon* and *Hart's War* followed, but so did the psychological chiller *The Sixth Sense.* "Bruce is one of the few actors who can play a rugged guy who is also dealing with emotions," said *Sixth Sense* writer-director M. Night Shyamalan. A classic example of art imitating life? Within a short time he was to see the end of his decade-long marriage to Demi Moore and to lose his brother Robert to cancer. But just three days after Robert's death, Willis staged a play in Hailey, Idaho, where Moore lives with their three children, and she attended. While his plunge back into the dating pool and his day job keep his name in headlines, Willis doesn't see a movie star when he faces the mirror. What he sees is "just a guy. Just a very fortunate guy."

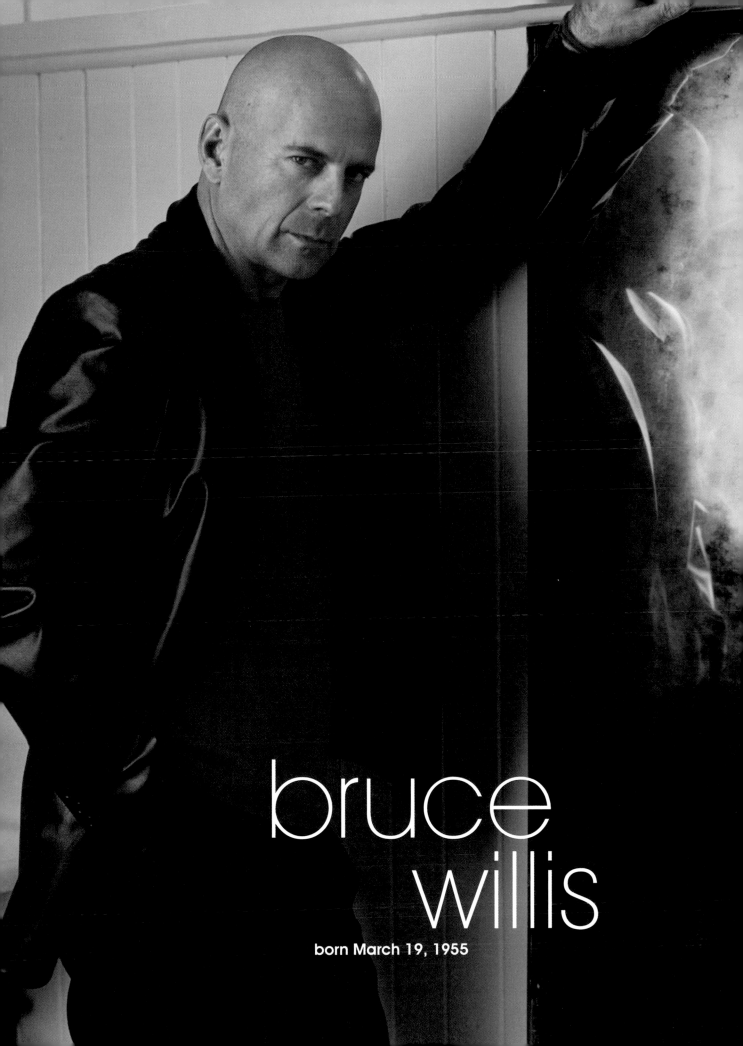

# bruce
## willis

born March 19, 1955

# arnold schwarzenegger

**born July 30, 1947**

He wasn't kidding when he said he'd be back. Arnold Schwarzenegger followed 1984's *The Terminator* with a deluge of testosterone-suffused hits, including *Commando, Predator, Total Recall* and the cyborgian sequel in 1991. "Historically, people with big muscles only got as far as playing Hercules," marveled the Austrian-born bodybuilder and five-time Mr. Universe, who debuted in the dubbed dud *Hercules in New York.* "I didn't expect to go as far as I have." As director James Cameron once warned, "He's never gonna play a character where he sits around in an office and wrings his hands." Onscreen anyway. A Republican intruder in the Kennedy clan—he has four kids with TV journalist wife Maria Shriver—Schwarzenegger headed the Council on Physical Fitness in the first Bush Administration and sits on the board of New York City's Twin Towers Fund. "I am a product of this land of opportunities," he has said, signaling possible political ambitions. But he's not going to pass up *Terminator 3,* which is due in 2003 and will pay him a Hollywood record $30 million.

**A**udiences cheered as she mowed down the mother monster in 1986's *Aliens*—a sci-fi sequel that not only improved on the original *Alien* but also proved that Sigourney Weaver was a brainy Yale drama grad who could still kick butt. Some called her a she-Rambo, but the statuesque (5'11") Weaver insisted Lieutenant Ripley was a triumph of mind over muscle. "I play her like Henry V," she said. But what did we expect from the daughter of British actress Elizabeth Inglis and the late Sylvester "Pat" Weaver, creator of the *Today* and *Tonight* shows? "Sigourney is the one person who's shown us that you can do it all," said Winona Ryder. Indeed, her career is wide-reaching—from the steamy political drama *The Year of Living Dangerously* to the rollicking *Ghostbusters* to her Oscar-nominated roles in *Aliens, Gorillas in the Mist* and *Working Girl.* But it is at her Manhattan home with director husband Jim Simpson and daughter Charlotte, 12, that Weaver found the ultimate mother-protector role. "In contrast to the popular image of myself as an alien-stomping, gun-toting Amazon," she said, "I am actually a peaceful person at heart."

# sigourney weaver

**born October 8, 1949**

# pierce brosnan

## born May 16, 1952

Since he was cast in 1995's *Golden-Eye*, the impossibly dashing Irishman from remote County Meath has found James Bond's Brioni dinner jacket a perfect fit. Pierce Brosnan "was a natural," said Barbara Broccoli, coproducer of his four 007 films. "He was trained in England, so he has the British sensibilities. He also has rugged good looks, the charm and the acting ability." Audiences seem to agree that TV's old Remington Steele is the most compelling Bond since Sean Connery, propelling the franchise to new box office highs. In private life Brosnan is a poster guy for domesticity, explaining, "Bedding and kissing some of the most beautiful women on-screen, I get to play it out so I have no need to do it offscreen." In 2001 he wed his longtime love and the mother of his two youngest sons (Dylan, 5, and Paris, 1), former broadcast journalist Keely Shaye Smith. Brosnan's first wife, actress Cassandra Harris, died in 1991 at 39 of ovarian cancer. They had a son, Sean, 18, and Brosnan adopted Cassie's children, Charlotte and Christopher. Brosnan is a close, involved dad, not least because his own father walked out when he was 2. "Having not known my dad," he says, "I suppose that's why I enjoy family life so much." Professionally Brosnan savors his non-Bond roles (*The Thomas Crown Affair, The Tailor of Panama*) but isn't leaving Her Majesty's Secret Service just yet. "I'd like to keep doing Bond as long as I can be plausible in the role, physically," he said. "You can get away with being older in close-ups, but then you have to fight and run." Or call the stuntman.

# AMERICA'S

**They're sassy, not saccharine, and, as one of them exulted, we like them, we *like* them!**

## meg ryan

**born November 19, 1961**

he said it best herself. "Through Clinton and Monica, Clinton and Hillary, the scandal, the impeachment, Iraq, Bruce and Demi, Ellen and Anne, I have remained consistently and nauseatingly adorable." Skewering her own gooey image, Meg Ryan declared, "I have, in fact, been known to cause diabetes." But the moviegoing public remained unshakably adoring of the former homecoming queen from Connecticut as she romped through romantic comedies, sugarcoating even bawdy moments like that famous faked orgasm in *When Harry Met Sally . . .* "She is *shockingly* inventive," said writer-director Nora Ephron, and the leading man she paired with Ryan in *Sleepless in Seattle* and *You've Got Mail* confirmed admiringly that it's all a brilliant act. "She is not 'pert' or 'perky' or soft at all," said Tom Hanks. "Meg is not to be messed around with." Her forays outside the rom-com genre tended to impress critics more than ticket buyers. On the South American set of one of those detours—the 2000 political drama *Proof of Life*—Ryan met and began a hugely trumpeted affair with her Australian costar Russell Crowe, 38. The pair are now just pals, but the tryst led to the breakup of her nine-year marriage to Dennis Quaid, 48 (they share custody of son Jack, now 10)—and a newfound sense of possibilities. "It's been terrifying, awful . . . and exhilarating," admitted Ryan. "When I look at my life, I'm very happy."

# SWEETHEARTS

# sandra bullock

born July 26, 1964

Sandra Bullock took the most direct route into America's heart—behind the wheel of a booby-trapped bus in 1994's *Speed*. Born in Virginia but a frequent traveler to Europe with her opera-singer mom, Bullock was determined to be "the girl nobody can quite figure out." Yet soon enough the public had Bullock pegged as the adorably plucky, coltishly klutzy heroine they saw in *While You Were Sleeping*. "She's not comfortable being a glamor-puss, so she goes for the comedy," observed Peter Bogdanovich, who directed her in *The Thing Called Love*. Then Bullock relocated to Austin, Texas, and switched to edgier roles. As a joint-smoking free spirit in 1999's *Forces of Nature*, she "wanted to challenge the image she had as an innocent," said costar Ben Affleck. A year later she made *Miss Congeniality* but no longer felt compelled to live up to the title off-screen. "When you've been around a bit, doing that cute, fresh thing would be faking it," remarked Bullock. "It would be pretending that I'm that person, and I'm not anymore."

A proper debutante from Nashville, Reese Witherspoon was dubbed Little Type A for her determination by her surgeon father and nursing-professor mother. Fast-forward to Hollywood a decade later and "she's superwoman," said *Legally Blonde* director Robert Luketic. "Very few people can do what Reese does—marriage, motherhood and a successful career. It's fantastic what she juggles at such a young age." Settled in L.A. with actor husband Ryan Phillippe, 27, Witherspoon has found daughter Ava, 2, "the ulti-mate dose of reality." But since starring at 14 in the coming-of-age film *The Man in the Moon*, the actress greets challenge, she has said, with "the personality of a Yorkshire terrier." Critics loved her in *Election, Pleasantville* and *Cruel Intentions*, and some have tabbed her the next Julia Roberts. Witherspoon did prove she could open a picture with the sleeper 2001 hit *Legally Blonde*, which debuted at No. 1 and earned $95 million on an $18 million budget. "There's a lot of pressure in being the kind of person that can carry a movie," she said. "I don't even know what that means yet. But I feel up to it."

# reese witherspoon

**born March 22, 1976**

T he public responds to Goldie," said pal and *First Wives Club* costar Diane Keaton. "There's only a handful of people who are adored, and Goldie is one of them." It was her infectious giggle—and dollops of body paint— that started the Goldie Hawn bandwagon on TV's *Laugh-In,* and her smarts kept it rolling. "I have a light personality and a deep-thinking brain," said the Washington, D.C.-born actress. After a Best Supporting Oscar for 1969's *Cactus Flower,* she helped pave the way for women in film by producing and starring in the successful *Private Benjamin.* "We need people like her to lift our spirits," said her *Everyone Says I Love You* castmate Alan Alda. "There's always a lot of laughing and fun with Goldie." Twice-divorced, Hawn lives in L.A. with longtime love Kurt Russell, 51, with whom she has raised four children, including actors Kate, 23, and Oliver, 25 (with second husband Bill Hudson). At home she's just Mom—albeit with sparkle. As Oliver once described her, she's "a lot like she is in her movies—like champagne, bubbly and floating."

# goldie hawn

born November 21, 1945

## drew barrymore

**born February 22, 1975**

At age 6, an adorable Drew Barrymore nearly upstaged an equally adorable alien in Steven Spielberg's blockbuster *E.T.*, and at this year's 20th-anniversary rerelease she called it "the grandest experience of my life." The cherubic heiress to the Barrymore acting dynasty proceeded to grow up in the public eye, working her considerable charms in otherwise lackluster fare like *Firestarter* and *Irreconcilable Differences*. Few knew she was also battling drug and alcohol abuse. "I think she conquered many demons early in life," said her *Batman Forever* director Joel Schumacher. "The nice thing about Drew is she's gotten strong but not tough." As Barrymore put it, "I am Miss Bubbly. But life is beautiful." Her love life, however, proved less so, and she has weathered brief failed marriages to Jeremy Thomas and Tom Green. "The hardships Drew has endured have made her the person she is today," said Jenno Topping, executive producer of *Charlie's Angels,* which Barrymore starred in and produced. "Resilient and full of fun. She is an uncontrollable, fearless force."

# sally field

**born November 6, 1946**

W hat's not to like? Beginning with her popular 1965 TV show *Gidget,* Sally Field surfed her way into the heart of America. "I was just as cute as I could possibly be," she later grimaced. But after starring in *The Flying Nun,* she began to hit higher notes in films. Following the rollicking 1977 hit *Smokey and the Bandit,* costarring then boyfriend Burt Reynolds, she earned an Oscar as a union organizer in *Norma Rae.* Her second Best Actress win (accepted with that indelible "You like me!" speech) was for 1984's *Places in the Heart.* "In all honesty, the one I want to emulate every time I go before the camera is Sally Field," said Tom Hanks, her *Punchline* and *Forrest Gump* costar. "I think she's a genius." She took fewer roles in the '90s to spend time with son Sam, now 14, by producer ex-husband Alan Greisman. (She also has two grown sons from her first marriage.) Then, last year, she won an Emmy for a guest spot on *ER* before starring as a Supreme Court justice on ABC's short-lived *The Court.* One of the perks of getting older is that she can play against her perky stereotype. As Field phrased it, "I hate that spunky thing."

Rarely does an actress debut with such a splash. Winning the first role she auditioned for, as a sexy nightclub performer in 1994's *The Mask,* former model Cameron Diaz danced her way to stardom. Critic Roger Ebert called her "a true discovery in the film, a genuine sex bomb with a gorgeous face, a wonderful smile and a gift of comic timing." Though Diaz, who is dating actor Jared Leto, 30, plays down her looks on occasion—most memorably as a frizzy brunette pet-shop owner in *Being John Malkovich* ("Why not try everything?" she said)—she's at her best when flaunting them in films like *Charlie's Angels* and *There's Something About Mary.* Even with her hair spiked by that gross-out gag in *Mary,* she came across as totally adorable. Known for her healthy appetite, athletic prowess and goofball guffaw, Diaz "is as close to the ideal woman as you can get," said *Mary* director Bobby Farrelly. "She's a whirlwind, a lightning rod . . . and an undeniable babe."

# cameron diaz

born August 30, 1972

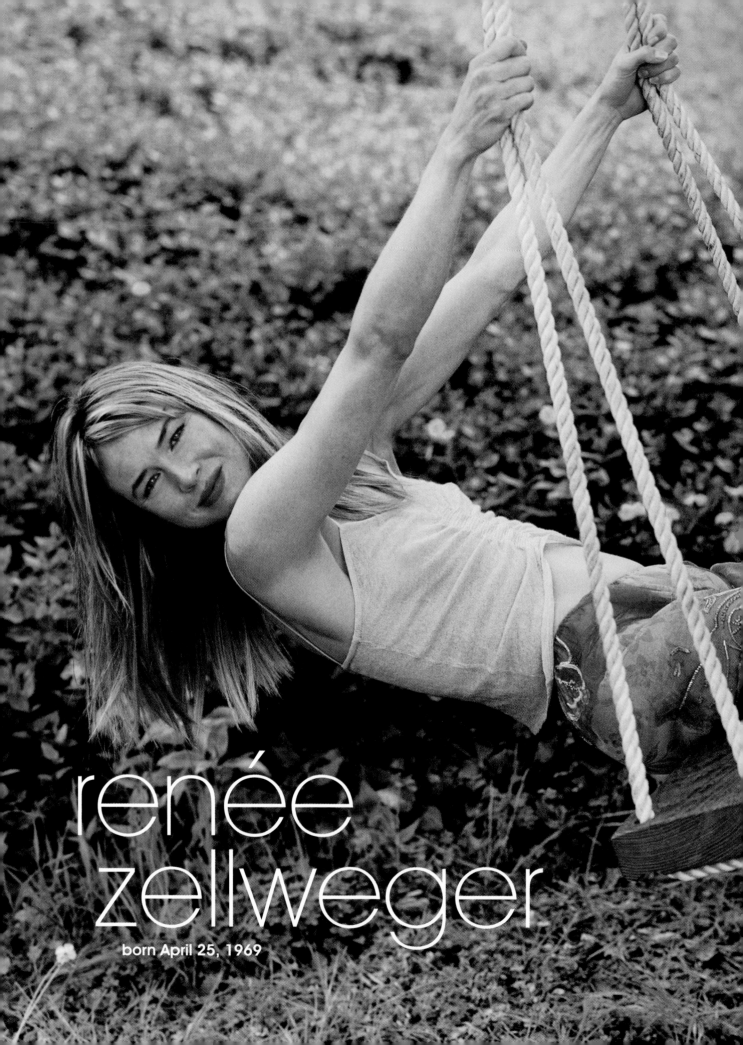

rénée
zellweger

born April 25, 1969

When the Texas native was cast as born-and-bred Brit diarist Bridget Jones, Americans and Londoners alike spat out their tea. But mastering a spot-on accent (and putting on 20 lbs.) for the role, Renée Zellweger not only pulled it off but also earned an Oscar nomination. She in fact added a degree of vulnerability to the character that the book was barely able to convey, and, as *Diary* author Helen Fielding observed, "Renée has a realness and sweetness that you probably can't act." Her sense of ease, coupled with her wide-eyed look of wonderment, impressed director Cameron Crowe into casting her over many better known auditioners for 1996's *Jerry Maguire*. "She reminds you of a sister, a friend, someone you were in love with once or now," said Crowe of her appeal as the girl-next-door who pined for Tom Cruise. "You don't feel ho-hum about her." As Zellweger's *Me, Myself & Irene* costar Jim Carrey, who dated the actress for a year after the film wrapped, once explained, "She's the person everyone would want to fall in love with." Single since their late-2000 breakup, Zellweger was awarded for her many charms last year when she won a Golden Globe for playing a mentally unbalanced waitress in *Nurse Betty*. As for her own role in Hollywood, she's becoming increasingly secure. "I am finally coming to a point where I can look at my life as more than an accident," she recently confessed. "I can look at it and say, I love what I do, and I'm lucky to get to do what I love."

THE

# WILD ONES

## Unpredictable, intense, they sell tickets ticking like time bombs

# sean penn

## born August 17, 1960

man of extremes—extreme talent, extreme mood swings—Sean Penn burst forth in 1982's *Fast Times at Ridgemont High* as a hilarious stoner with an outlook as sunny as the film's Southern California setting. With few exceptions, the actor thought of as perhaps the finest of his generation wouldn't be seen smiling again for two decades. Onscreen, Penn specialized in complex, often unlikable souls as in *Casualties of War* and *Hurlyburly,* and in his blistering Oscar-nominated role as a condemned death row killer in 1995's *Dead Man Walking.* "He had a rage, I think, an addiction to rage," said *Dead* costar Susan Sarandon, a Penn pal. "Sometimes people were just afraid of him." Though capable of great charm, he generated fear offscreen, too, punctuating his tempestuous four-year marriage to Madonna (who called him "a cowboy poet") with fistfights with photographers and a 30-day jail stint for assaulting a film extra. He moved into directing with *The Indian Runner* in 1991, the same year he began a relationship with actress Robin Wright (*The Princess Bride*), now 36, which has led to two children, a 1996 marriage and a seeming newfound sense of calm. Though smiling radiantly through much of his latest Oscar-nominated role as the mentally challenged hero of the 2001 weepie *I Am Sam,* Penn once confessed, "I'm not going to accuse myself of being happy. Just saying that would put me in a bad mood. But I am feeling productive. There's a lot of good things going on."

# johnny depp

born June 9, 1963

Count on Johnny Depp to be captain of his own soul and career path. "I'm not Blockbuster Boy; I never wanted to be," he once declared. He'd rather pursue film's artsier, edgier fringe than just maximize the box office potential of his razor-sharp cheekbones and luscious bad-boy pout. Typical choices for the much tattooed, Florida-bred high school dropout were the endearing freak that was *Edward Scissorhands* and the cross-dressing Z-movie director in *Ed Wood.* "Everyone in film respects him. No one can predict what weird role he'll show up in next," said John Waters, his director in the satire *Cry-Baby.* "He'll be 80 and still surprising audiences." After years of wild-child headlines (a trashed hotel suite, paparazzi scuffles) and a string of high-profile engagements—including to Winona Ryder and Jennifer Grey—the guitar-playing owner of L.A.'s Viper Room finally settled down in Paris with French singer-actress Vanessa Paradis, 29, and their two children. After the first, Lily-Rose, was born in 1999, "I looked at her and instantly everything came into sharp focus," he reflected. "Everything else is just Parcheesi."

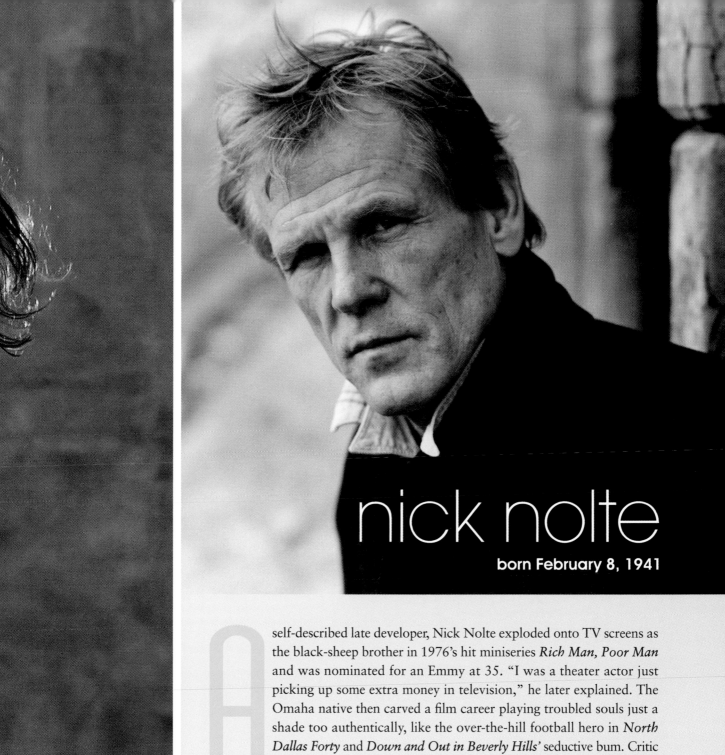

# nick nolte

**born February 8, 1941**

A self-described late developer, Nick Nolte exploded onto TV screens as the black-sheep brother in 1976's hit miniseries *Rich Man, Poor Man* and was nominated for an Emmy at 35. "I was a theater actor just picking up some extra money in television," he later explained. The Omaha native then carved a film career playing troubled souls just a shade too authentically, like the over-the-hill football hero in *North Dallas Forty* and *Down and Out in Beverly Hills'* seductive bum. Critic Pauline Kael once called him "a master of the mixed-up." His life provided plenty of inspiration: a felony (a five-year suspended sentence in 1962 for selling fake draft cards), alcoholism, drug use, three divorces and a palimony suit. His Oscar-nominated performance as the tortured Tom Wingo in *The Prince of Tides* led to a string of big-bucks projects—like *I Love Trouble,* with Julia Roberts—before a switch back to more artful independent works. "It's not about the movie business for him now," said Sissy Spacek, his costar in *Affliction,* which brought his second Oscar nomination. "He's been there and he's done that." These days are about being with son Brawley, 16, from his third marriage, and doing smaller films that interest him regardless of the financial reward. As Nolte put it, "It's kind of a reconnection for me—you don't need 15 Mercedes, do you?"

# robert
# de niro

born August 17, 1943

**H**e spoke only 17 words of English in *Godfather II*. The rest Robert De Niro delivered in Italian so perfect it fooled even *paisani*, but the script was the very least of the power of his performance. "You don't need words to express feeling; a grunt can do more than two paragraphs, or even just a look," said the minimalist master, who climbed so deeply into characters like *The King of Comedy*'s delusional Rupert Pupkin and *Taxi Driver*'s deranged sociopath Travis Bickle ("You talkin' to me?") that the real De Niro remained virtually unknowable. "My joy as an actor is to live different lives without risking the real-life consequences," explained the inscrutable, press-shy star hailed as the heir to Brando. De Niro did have to put on 60 lbs. to play aging pug Jake La Motta in Martin Scorsese's mesmerizing *Raging Bull*, a portrayal which won him a second Oscar. "He has set the standard for generations to come," cheered fellow tough-guy actor and *Mean Streets* costar Harvey Keitel. Then, in recent years, De Niro helped found a film center and several hot restaurants in his gritty downtown Manhattan neighborhood, and branched into comedy. The father of five (by three different women) razzed his past in *Meet the Parents* and played off straight man Billy Crystal as a mobster having a meltdown in *Analyze This*. "People get older, they change. You open up or you close off," said Scorsese of his pal. "He opens."

# nicolas cage

### born January 7, 1964

I s it Method or madness? He ate a live cockroach for one role, had two teeth extracted sans novocaine to feel the pain of a Vietnam vet in another and holed up in a hotel room with a vodka bottle to get into the psyche of a suicidal alcoholic in 1995's *Leaving Las Vegas*. That last part earned him an Oscar if only $240,000, but the price of Nicolas Cage was on its way to the present $20 million per picture. He is versatile. When not doing his walking-land-mine bit, he can deliver droopy-eyed charm or hit lighter notes, as he proved in *Honeymoon in Vegas, Raising Arizona* and, opposite Cher, in the romantic classic *Moonstruck*. Determined to succeed on his own rather than through any connection with Francis Ford Coppola, his famed director uncle, he concocted a surname honoring avant-garde composer John Cage and comic-book character Luke Cage. But he's not opposed to commerce. "We're in an entertainment industry," Cage has observed. "It's not just putting on the beret and smoking a Gitane and saying, 'I'm only going to do foreign films because I'm erudite and I'm so cool.'" That explains his penchant for bang-'em-up blockbusters like *The Rock, Con Air* and *Face/Off*. Yet he does add distinction to the genre. "Nic brings a more character-driven sense to the action hero, a little darker, more complicated and conversational," Sylvester Stallone once noted. Cage, who was married to Patricia Arquette for nearly six years and then dated Lisa Marie Presley, has a son, Weston, 11, with former girlfriend Christina Fulton. If David Lynch hadn't already done a film called *Wild at Heart*, starring Cage, that could be the title of his own bioflick. "A lot of edgy's coming out of me, man," he has said. "You've heard of wall-to-wall carpet? This is wall-to-wall edge."

# samuel l. jackson

### born December 21, 1948

**M**uch like Shaft, whom he played in 2000, Samuel L. Jackson is ready to roll when duty calls. "Sam can be sitting around joking, but when you say 'Action' he becomes the most intense and focused actor," said Joel Schumacher, his director in *A Time to Kill.* "I've never seen anyone with the facility to transform himself that quickly." Indeed, Jackson shot more films than any other Hollywood actor in the '90s, the decade in which he found his career and saved his life. When he came to Spike Lee's set to play a crack addict in 1991's *Jungle Fever,* he had been one himself—and was, in fact, just two weeks out of rehab. Jackson won a Cannes Film Festival award for that chilling performance and followed up four years later with an Oscar nomination as an Ezekiel-spieling, Jheri-Kurled hit man in *Pulp Fiction.* The culmination for him was donning the robe of a Jedi Master in 1999's *Star Wars: Episode I—The Phantom Menace.* "All of a sudden I'm standing on a set doing scenes with Yoda," he marveled. "I said to myself, 'I've arrived.' " Sharing his satisfaction was actress LaTanya Richardson, his costar in *Losing Isaiah* and wife of 22 years, and their daughter Zoe, 20. There is only one problem Samuel L. Jackson hasn't solved as yet, and time for it is written into all of his film contracts. "Golf," he joked, "is my new drug."

# anthony hopkins

**born December 31, 1937**

He staked his place in the zeitgeist as perhaps the scariest screen monster of our era, winning an Oscar as the suave, brilliant and voracious cannibal Hannibal Lecter in 1991's *The Silence of the Lambs*. "I played Lecter with great relish," said Welsh-born Anthony Hopkins, who has broadcast bluntly that he is happier in Hollywood than on the British stage, where for 20 years he was touted as the next Olivier. In theater, "you have to be a team player, and I'm not good at that," allowed the self-described loner, who channeled his demons into three indelible roles in the mid-'90s: the title characters in *Nixon* and *Surviving Picasso,* and the quietly desperate butler in *The Remains of the Day.* Knighted by the Queen in 1993 and adding U.S. citizenship in 2000, he lives in L.A. He had a daughter by a first marriage, and this year saw the end of his second union, after 29 years, to Jenni Lynton, who described him as "a seething mass of contradictions, almost impossible to understand." Any such mystery does not affect his art. "It's as if he thinks the thoughts of Picasso or Nixon, and his face transforms into Picasso or Nixon," marveled pal Julia Roberts. "It's just the best party trick I've ever seen."

# STAR BURSTS

## With celestial casting, this cluster entered the film firmament

# bo derek

### born November 20, 1956

he was in the movie *10* for barely 10 minutes, but Bo Derek just as quickly became the new symbol of beauty in America. With her taut figure, her tawny skin and—who could forget?—her blonde cornrowed hair, her image sold over 500,000 posters in just the first month after the 1979 release of the film. "It was like the Beatles and *A Hard Day's Night*," she said. "People used to start running down the street, and by the time they get to you it's a huge mob. It was that insane." Mary Cathleen Collins was a model when she met actor John Derek at 16 (he was married to Linda Evans at the time), and became his fourth wife in 1976. Despite very little experience, she was a natural in the role of Dudley Moore's perfect woman. Her Svengali-like husband later directed her in a couple of larger parts (*Tarzan, the Ape Man* and *Bolero*), but they did nothing for audiences, or her career. In 1995, though, she made a memorable return to the screen as Chris Farley's foxy stepmother in *Tommy Boy*. John, 30 years Bo's senior, died of heart failure in 1998, and the actress is still adjusting to life without him. Some things, however, never change. As John's second wife Ursula Andress, a close friend of Bo's, recently said, "She was a 10 then, and she's a 10 today."

diane
keaton

born January 5, 1946

With a rumpled-chic wardrobe and a disarming flair for comedy, Diane Keaton la-di-da'ed her way to an Oscar as the lovable neurotic Annie Hall in the 1977 film. "Diane is always totally surprised when people find her amusing," said her *Hall* director, costar and then boyfriend, Woody Allen. "She is a natural comedienne, but she never quite believes she can do it." The L.A. native had done it in three earlier Allen films, but it was *Hall* that earned her critical kudos —along with a brand-new pigeonhole. Of course, as she later said, "How could I resent *Annie Hall*, the thing that gave me all I have? Yes, I got typecast. Yes, I lost my privacy—but God, give me that again!" The typecasting turned out not to restrict her, as she proved with Best Actress nominations for *Reds* and *Marvin's Room*. The never-wed mother of adoptive daughter Dexter, 6, and son Duke, 19 months, turned her attention in the '80s to directing (*Heaven, Unstrung Heroes*). Yet acting remains her "bread and butter," she said recently, adding, "Life is too short for missed opportunities."

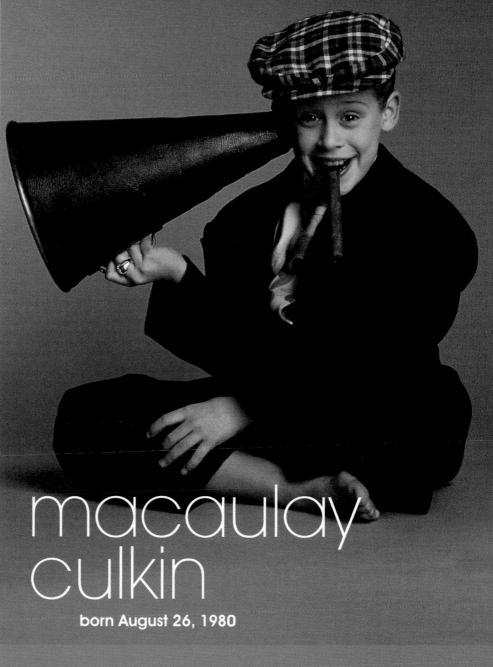

# macaulay culkin

## born August 26, 1980

He was prince of the world at 10, the adorable towheaded hero of *Home Alone* and en route to becoming the highest-paid kid star ever with his $8 million take for 1994's *Richie Rich*. Macaulay Culkin "had more presence than any child actor I can remember since Shirley Temple," said David Friendly, who cast him in 1991's *My Girl*. But, burned out from the grind imposed by his manager father, Culkin quit acting at 14. The following year, a grueling custody battle erupted between his parents, Kit Culkin and Patricia Brentrup, over their seven kids. (She won.) At 17—a year before coming into his $17 million trust—he ventured into the adult role of husband to actress Rachel Miner, also 17. Separated two years later, he braved the London stage in *Madame Melville*, earning raves as a 15-year-old seduced by his French teacher. "It feels weird to be back," admitted the reclusive New Yorker, who prepared this year to return to film as a cross-dressing murderer in *Party Monster*. "But it feels good."

# kathleen turner

born June 19, 1954

Assuming she was just another Wasp without a sting in her tail, studio brass resisted casting Kathleen Turner as the murderous seductress in 1981's *Body Heat*. But a dazzling audition led to a sizzling movie debut as man-eater Matty Walker and to comparisons with an unrelated earlier Turner—Lana. Kathleen had the sophistication of a diplomat's daughter who had grown up around the world and a sultry contralto that could bring off lines like "You're not very bright, are you? I like that in a man." Not to mention long lovely legs and what Steve Martin called "a behind you'd like to eat lunch off." Later Turner proved she had more than flesh to peddle in such films as *The Man*

*with Two Brains, Prizzi's Honor* and *Peggy Sue Got Married*. "Kathleen can do it all," said Michael Douglas, her costar in *Romancing the Stone*. "She's funny, sexy, vulnerable and endlessly intriguing, because you never know which side she's going to show you next." She married New York City real estate mogul Jay Weiss in 1984, and they have a daughter, Rachel, 14. Gamely fighting rheumatoid arthritis for the past decade, she recently returned to her temptress roots—playing Mrs. Robinson in a stage adaptation of the Anne Bancroft-Dustin Hoffman film classic *The Graduate*. Her nightly nude scene at age 47 was a reminder of Turner's enduring sexual confidence. "I always want to accept a dare, to try something," she said. Somewhere, Matty Walker must be smiling.

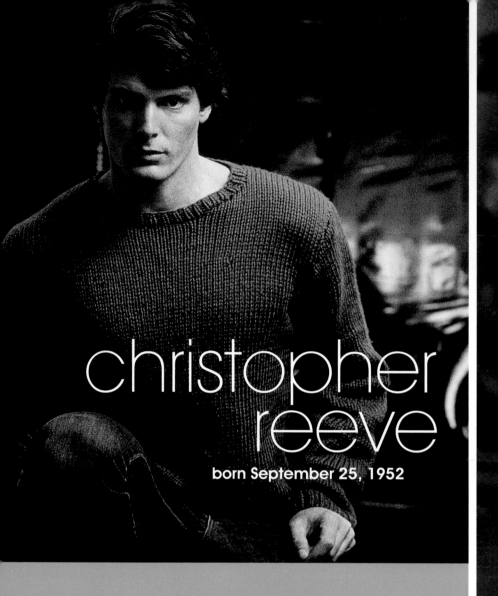

# christopher reeve

### born September 25, 1952

"What makes Superman a hero," Christopher Reeve observed, "is not that he has power but that he has the wisdom and maturity to use the power wisely." After soaring to fame as the Man of Steel in 1978's *Superman* and its three sequels, Reeve himself became a role model. Thrown from his horse during a 1995 equestrian event, the Juilliard-trained actor was paralyzed from the neck down. Initially, he was scared of the battle ahead. "Maybe we should let me go," he said to wife Dana, 41, mom to his son Will, 10. (Reeve also has two grown children with a former girlfriend.) But he now uses his star clout to raise money and awareness for spinal-cord research. "It's not a job I would have chosen," he said, "but one that I fully embrace." Since the accident, Reeve has starred in a TV remake of *Rear Window* and penned a bestselling memoir, *Still Me*. "He will be the father of spinal-cord regeneration for all time," said pal Mandy Patinkin. "I think God sent Chris to be the man to do this because of his heart and courage and fight. He's more than Superman."

Born into a showbiz brood of seven—Mom was actress Maureen O'Sullivan, Dad was director John Farrow—Mia Farrow was always more drawn to family than fame. "I never really plotted a career," she admitted. Following TV's *Peyton Place* and a fast and fiery marriage, at 21, to the 50-year-old Chairman of the Board, Frank Sinatra, she broke through in 1968's *Rosemary's Baby* but soon shunned the spotlight to wed maestro André Previn and start a family. Seven children (three biological) and one divorce later, she emerged as Woody Allen's muse, effortlessly morphing from New Yawk cigarette girl (*Radio Days*) to calm, moral center in a sea of dysfunction (*Hannah and Her Sisters*). "She's an extraordinary actress," Allen once said of his partner of 12 years. "And she's real sweet." But it ended bitterly in 1992 when the mother of 14 learned Allen was in love with—and would eventually wed—her adoptive daughter Soon-Yi, and refused him access to the children. Surviving the ugly public heartbreak, she has found peace in New York City, working only occasionally. "I have this wonderful family," she said. "I am really, truly blessed."

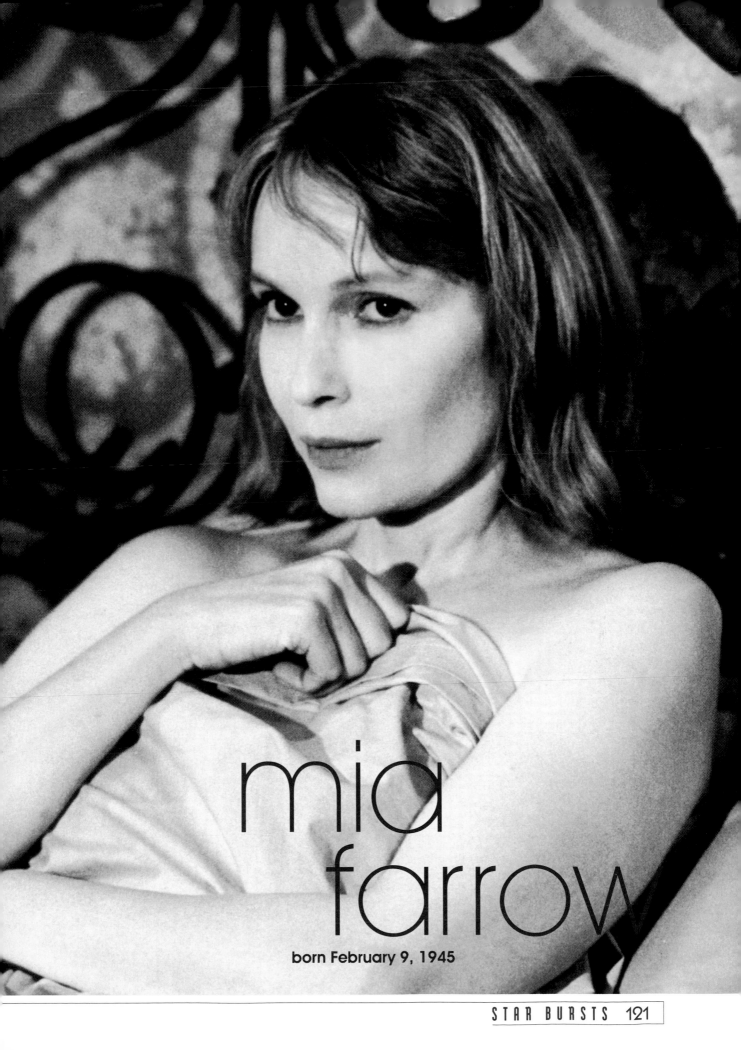

mia
farrow

born February 9, 1945

urt Reynolds became one of the first actors to leap successfully from TV (*Dan August*) to movie superstardom. For the onetime stuntman, *Cosmo* centerfold and son of a Florida police chief, 1972's tumultuous white-water drama *Deliverance* was "a once-in-a-lifetime chance to establish myself as a serious actor." Follow-up hits *Semi-Tough, Starting Over* and, particularly, the *Smokey and the Bandit* series made him Hollywood's No. 1 draw from 1978 to 1982. But mid-decade the roguish good ol' boy began an epic nosedive. "He had all this talent," rued *Deliverance* castmate Jon Voight. "He didn't appreciate his own gift." The free fall accelerated in 1984, when he developed TMJ (temporomandibular joint disorder) and dropped to 140 lbs. A 1991 Emmy for *Evening Shade* was his sole career redemption, and his romantic life was a highly public shambles. Flameouts included first wife Judy Carne, Dinah Shore, Chris Evert and *Bandit* costar Sally Field. His megawatt second marriage to Loni Anderson ended rancorously in 1993 following his affair with cocktail-lounge manager Pam Seals, 46, who remains with him today. Then a custody battle over adopted son Quinton, now 13, helped put him into bankruptcy. In 1997 he rose from the ashes (and got an Oscar nomination) playing a porn king in *Boogie Nights*. Said Reynolds: "I know I'll never be No. 1 again, but I'll be a working actor. And this time I'll be a grown-up."

# burt reynolds

born February 11, 1936

# CLOWNS

## In the kill-or-die craft of comedy, all hail these artful killers

# jim carrey

### born January 17, 1962

For 15 years he worked comedy clubs, Vegas and TV shows like *In Living Color,* but such stages were like cages for the Canadian-born dervish. It took film to finally set him free. In *Ace Ventura: Pet Detective,* Carrey cut loose with his spring-hinged limbs and Silly Putty face, and enjoyed a sleeper blockbuster. Jerry Lewis hailed him as "the best physical comedian to have come down the pike in a hundred years," and Carrey, a high school dropout at 16 after his dad lost his job, became the most bankable movie buffoon since Robin Williams—and the first to earn $20 million for a role (1996's *The Cable Guy*). In the late 1990s he made his mark as a serious actor in the satirical *Truman Show* and *Man on the Moon,* a biopic of comic Andy Kaufman. "Underneath him, there is a lot of depth," noted *Moon* costar Courtney Love. "And a lot of sexiness . . . in a sort of deep, soulful and almost dark way." "I can smile my way through life if I want to, but I don't want to," admitted Carrey, who has a daughter, 14, with first wife Melissa Womer and was divorced from actress Lauren Holly in 1997. In 2000's *Me, Myself and Irene,* he was bouncing off the walls again but determined not to be a joker lifer. "If you ever hear that I signed up to do *Ace Ventura 5,*" he told an interviewer, "call me up and remind me to put a bullet in my head, okay?"

# mike myers

born May 25, 1963

"I can't split the atom, I can't row a boat, and I don't know Esperanto," Mike Myers once said. "Everything else I can do." Such chutzpah is forgivable from the guy who wrote the original 1997 *Austin Powers* script in just three weeks, creating an unlikely movie mega-franchise based on a snaggletoothed, furry-chested dim-Brit spy and introducing the term "shagadelic" to the pop-culture vernacular. "It's rare to use words like 'comic genius' with any meaningfulness," said Michael York, the seasoned British actor who plays Austin's boss, Basil Exposition. "But it's justified." Raised in a Toronto suburb, Myers joined the Second City comedy troupe just hours after his final high school exam. Later, at *Saturday Night Live,* he developed memorable characters like the often farklemt Linda Richman (based on the mother of his wife, comedy writer Robin Ruzan, 38) and party-hearty teen Wayne Campbell, star of Myers's first film smash, *Wayne's World.* The voice of *Shrek* last year, Myers hopes his latest and third Powers picture, *Goldmember,* will lead to a Bond-like run. Groovy, baby.

# woody allen

**born December 1, 1935**

The glasses. The whine. The hypochondria. The tweedy Jewish neurotic intellectual. Woody Allen is as instantly identifiable as the Empire State Building in the skyline of his beloved Manhattan. As an actor, "I have an incredibly limited range," admitted America's premier auteur and a three-time Oscar winner. "What I can do, I can do, but ask me to go beyond that—say, to play in Chekhov—and it'd be preposterous." Chekhov, shmekhov. Bring on *Annie Hall*'s lobster-phobic comic, the hapless talent agent of *Broadway Danny Rose* or the hesitant sperm in *Everything You Wanted to Know About Sex*. "He *is* his premise" for comedy, said *Saturday Night Live* producer Lorne Michaels, who once crafted jokes for Allen, himself originally a writer for Sid Caesar. Shockingly sad family matters made headlines in 1992, when Allen disclosed his involvement with Soon-Yi Previn, then 21, the adopted daughter of his longtime love and costar, Mia Farrow. Having lost custody of the son and daughter he adopted with Farrow, as well as the biological son they had, Allen made Previn his third wife in 1997, adopted two more daughters and continued to turn out a movie a year.

I

f I ever see a path I haven't gone on," Whoopi Goldberg once remarked, "I'll walk down it." True to her
bravado, the onetime welfare mother has trod some di-
vergent paths—including bricklaying and mortuary
cosmetology—en route to becoming one of the most
prolific and successful female comedians of her time.
She got there with her own unique assets—a lava flow
of dreadlocks, a honeyed rasp where her voice should be and
a name that's half exclamation point, half Jewish star. "Whoopi
is a trailblazer. The only problem is, she blazes the trail and
then takes the damn job!" actress Wanda Sykes joked at last
year's Kennedy Center ceremony awarding Goldberg the Mark
Twain Prize for American Humor. "Whoopi works too much."
Known originally for her outrageous stand-up act and brash
one-woman shows, New York City-born Caryn Elaine Johnson (she went Whoopi in her 20s; Goldberg was her mother's
suggestion) snagged an Oscar nomination for her 1985 feature film debut in *The Color Purple* and took home the Best
Supporting Actress trophy five years later for *Ghost*. She's still
taking all the jobs. In addition to acting, she executive-produced
and starred on the syndicated *Hollywood Squares* for four
seasons, cohosts (with Robin Williams and Billy Crystal) HBO's
annual Comic Relief to aid the homeless and has emceed the
Academy Awards four times. With three divorces behind her,
Goldberg, who lives in California's Pacific Palisades, is happy
to dote on daughter Alexandrea, 28, and her three grandkids.
Just don't expect this grandma to take to her rocker anytime
soon. "I want to laugh," she has proclaimed. "I want light-
ness in the world. I want it to be more fun."

# whoopi goldberg

**born November 13, 1955**

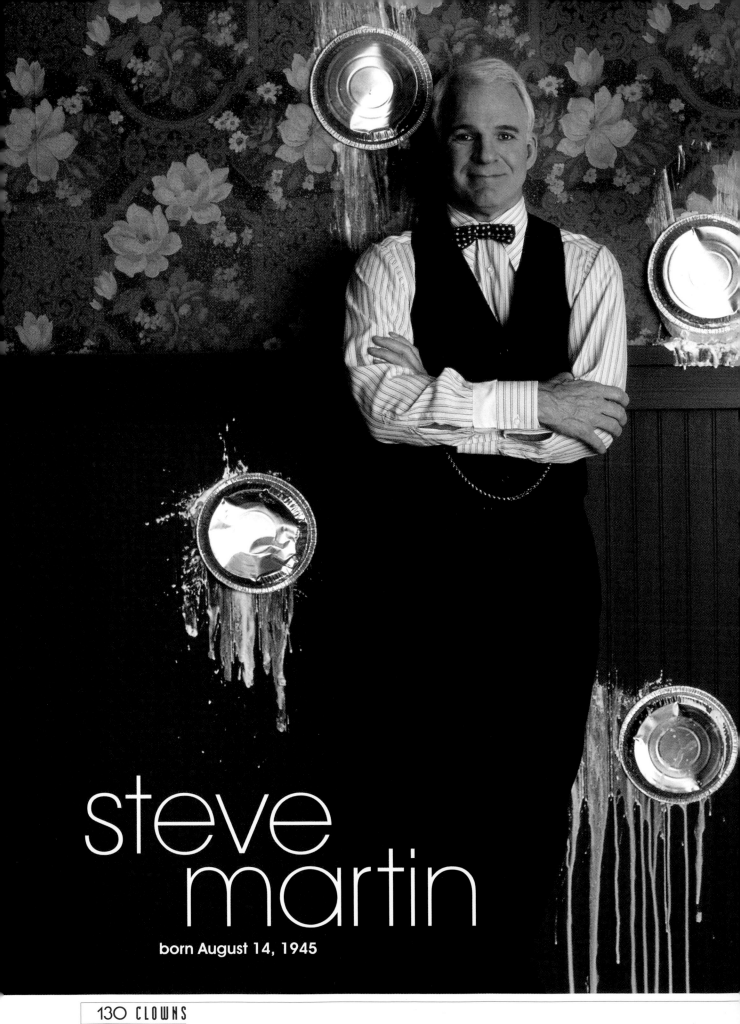

# steve martin

born August 14, 1945

How does a silver-haired stand-up best known for making balloon animals suddenly become a super-star with 20,000 fans screaming "Excuuuuse me"? For Steve Martin, the answer was hosting *Saturday Night Live*. "There was something about him and us that just clicked," said *SNL* producer Lorne Michaels. In his dozen encores, the former philosophy major unleashed King Tut and, with Dan Aykroyd, the wild-and-crazy Czech playboys. Observed Michaels: "Steve can play dim better than anyone." In 1979, the banjo-playing "Happy Feet" dancer waltzed into the movies with a gut-buster smash, *The Jerk,* and continued to charm audiences in two remakes, *Roxanne,* his version of Cyrano de Bergerac, and *Father of the Bride.* In private, Martin was shaken by the 1994 end of his seven-year marriage to *L.A. Story* costar Victoria Tennant and his subsequent self-described "torturous love affair" with Anne Heche. Now living quietly in L.A. and Santa Barbara, he has shifted increasingly into writing. "I'm not doing 'wild and crazy,' *The Man with Two Brains* comedy anymore," he noted. "If I didn't change, I'd be an idiot."

# adam sandler

**born September 9, 1966**

Rarely has dumb been so brilliant. Though savaged by critics, 1998's *The Waterboy* and *Big Daddy* the following year—both featuring Adam Sandler as a bumbling bonehead—earned more than $160 million each. "Adam's kind of the Everyman," said pal and fellow *Saturday Night Live* alum David Spade. That, of course, assumes that Everyman is a 12-year-old boy. "You feel smarter than him," continued Spade. "You feel sorry for him." Don't. Though Sandler, whose New Hampshire schoolteachers first bore the brunt of his jokes, briefly had to sing for his supper in the New York subways, he was hired at *SNL* by 1990. In five years there he left his sophomoric mark with his Canteen Boy and Opera Man characters. He soon cut two comedy albums that went platinum, and cowrote his first two farces, *Billy Madison* and *Happy Gilmore.* With his romantic turn in 1998's *The Wedding Singer* opposite Drew Barrymore, he became—unlikely as it seems—a major star. "I am not particularly smart. I am not particularly talented. I am not particularly good-looking," conceded Sandler. "And yet I am a multimillionaire."

# mel brooks

born June 28, 1926

I'm on the top of my game again," declared the comic-writer-director at 75, when *The Producers* became one of Broadway's all-time smashes. "I'm the real Mel Brooks once more." You remember Mel: the no-joke-is-too-low madcap madman behind such '70s comedy classics as *Blazing Saddles* and *Young Frankenstein*. Or the creator of the kid-pleasing romps *Spaceballs* and *Robin Hood: Men in Tights*. But in the '90s the air seemed to come out of the party balloon. Movies like *Life Stinks* bombed. Friends (notably *Catch-22* author Joseph Heller) began succumbing to old age. Brooks was "so full of angst," said actress Anne Bancroft, 70, his wife of 37 years, that "he was not funny." Then the curtain rose on *The Producers*, the 2001 stage remake of his 1968 cult film. Overnight, it was springtime for Brooks again. He won a Tony—elevating him to the elite ranks of those who have earned the grand slam of showbiz prizes: Oscar, Tony, Emmy, Grammy. "It's the most miraculous thing," said Carl Reiner, Brooks's partner on the hilarious *2000 Years* albums. Finally the Brooklyn-born father of four (two sons and a daughter with first wife Florence Baum, one son with Bancroft) had broken free of high anxiety and of fear of meeting the Great Ziegfeld in the sky. "If I die, I die. I'm making young friends," he said. "The hell with it! Let *them* lose me."

# eddie murphy

**born April 3, 1961**

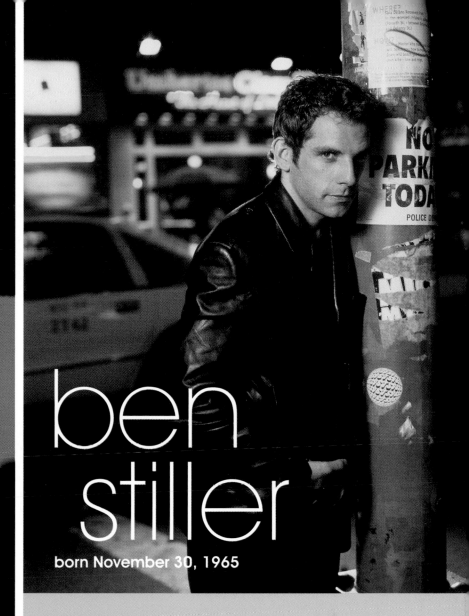

With a braying laugh and a mastery of edgy characters ("I'm Gumby, dammit!"), Eddie Murphy debuted as *Saturday Night Live*'s youngest trouper at 19 in 1980. He "blew us all away," said cast colleague Joe Piscopo. In the next few years Murphy started blowing away moviegoers as well in blockbusters like *48 HRS.* and *Beverly Hills Cop,* and found himself in the headlines, with tales of a ballooning ego and a jumbo-size entourage. "I don't think that entertainers should be heroes or preachers," he said at the time. By the early '90s, with his career stalled in a rut of sequels and duds, the bad-boy king of comedy started crafting a family-man image with kid-friendly hits like *The Nutty Professor* and *Dr. Dolittle.* He even put that hee-haw laugh to work again as the voice of Shrek's donkey sidekick in the 2001 animated smash. Living in the New Jersey suburbs with his wife of nine years, former model Nicole, 34, and their five kids (he also has two children from other relationships), Murphy is now a real-life family man. Said *Dolittle* producer John Davis: "The longer he is in show business, the more normal he gets."

# ben stiller

**born November 30, 1965**

The guy sure isn't afraid to make a fool of himself. But whether donning a garish tux with a troublesome zipper in *There's Something About Mary* or a barely-there Speedo in *Meet the Parents,* Ben Stiller "has a great balance of full-on physical sex appeal and a sense of disaster," said his *Parents* director Jay Roach. Stiller exploited both to full effect in his male-supermodel spoof *Zoolander,* which he wrote, directed and starred in. Unlike his narcissistic character, he said, "I have no problems with vanity when it comes to work." The son of comedy couple Jerry Stiller and Anne Meara, Ben had his own MTV sketch show in 1990 and later directed *Reality Bites* and *The Cable Guy.* But since *Mary,* he has spent more time in front of the camera. Most recently, he has been playing dad to his infant daughter, with wife Christine Taylor, 30, his *Zoolander* costar. "The great thing about having a real love in your life," he reflected, "is that they're there for you even when your movie hasn't made $100 million."

From nerd extraordinaire Todd DiLa-Muca dispensing noogies to Gilda Radner's Lisa Loopner on *Saturday Night Live* to pompous Polonius dispensing advice to son Laertes in 2000's modern-dress movie *Hamlet*, Bill Murray has enjoyed an audacious career. As *The New York Times* pronounced, "He is now perceived as an actor who also does comedy." Quite a feat for a man who told Columbia University School of the Arts' Class of 2000, "I just sort of got into acting to get out of the house. My mother was driving me nuts." After a start in Chicago's Second City company, he parlayed a three-year *SNL* stint into films, hitting it huge with *Caddyshack, Stripes, Ghostbusters* and *Groundhog Day,* as well as subtler successes like *Rushmore.* "When Bill's good, it's the same as when De Niro's good," said *SNL* producer Lorne Michaels. Murray resides in a New York City suburb with wife Jennifer, the mother of his three younger sons (he has two others from a first marriage). "I get a great feeling," he has said, "when my children are content and they're happy and they're proud."

# bill murray

**born September 21, 1950**

B₃ I₁ L₁ L₁

# billy crystal

**born March 14, 1948**

**B**ehind the twinkle in Billy Crystal's eye, there is always a glint of his classic *Saturday Night Live* creations: Fernando ("You look mahvelous!"), Willie ("I hate when that happens!") and a hundred other free spirits he has conjured in three decades of comedy. Of course, when Mr. Don't Get Me Started hit Hollywood pay dirt in 1989's *When Harry Met Sally . . .*, he unveiled a subtler, more sensitive side. "I'm basically a serious guy with a good sense of humor," the actor-writer-director-producer has said. And an *unbelieeewuble* gift for tapping into America's funny bone— from his saddled-up ad salesman in *City Slickers* to a "family" therapist in *Analyze This* to the voice of wisecracking one-eyed Mike Wazowski in *Monsters, Inc.* to seven peerless performances as host of the Academy Awards. "Billy is quick and agile and bright, and he plays the unexpected events of the telecast like a Stradivarius," said Oscar producer Gilbert Cates. Crystal often credits his stability to his Long Island sweetheart and wife of 32 years, Janice, with whom he has two daughters, Jennifer, 29, an actress, and Lindsay, 24, a filmmaker. "I fell in love with the right person," Crystal has said. "I still want to make her laugh."

obin Williams silent? Though he started out as a mime, the transplanted Midwesterner didn't keep his mouth shut for long in Hollywood. After he burst the confines of the small screen as a motormouthed free-associating alien on the sitcom *Mork & Mindy,* writer Larry Gelbart (*Tootsie*) dubbed him "the most amazing comedian of the last 25 years. He's like Groucho on speed. A giant." But following his movie breakthrough in 1982's *The World According to Garp,* Williams got lost in a haze of drugs and alcohol. Fortunately the imminent birth of his first child and the death of pal John Belushi scared him straight, and he rebounded, swooping up three Oscar nominations (*Good Morning, Vietnam, Dead Poets Society* and *The Fisher King*). His fourth proved the charm when he won Best Supporting Actor for 1997's *Good Will Hunting.* "People often overlook the fact that he's an incredible actor as well as a comedian," said Matt Damon, *Hunting*'s cowriter and costar. "They think he channels. In fact it's the culmination of such an extraordinary work ethic and effort." Williams lives in San Francisco with his second wife, Marsha Garces, 45, and children Zachary (with first wife Valerie Velardi), 19, Zelda, 12, and Cody, 10, but continues to do stand-up and to defy moviegoers' expectations, bouncing from mainstream megahit (*Mrs. Doubtfire*) to grim thriller (*Insomnia*). "He embraces the tragic and finds a cosmic sense of humor about it," says *Garp* costar Glenn Close. "With all the grief in the world, I thank God for Robin."

# robin williams

born July 21, 1951

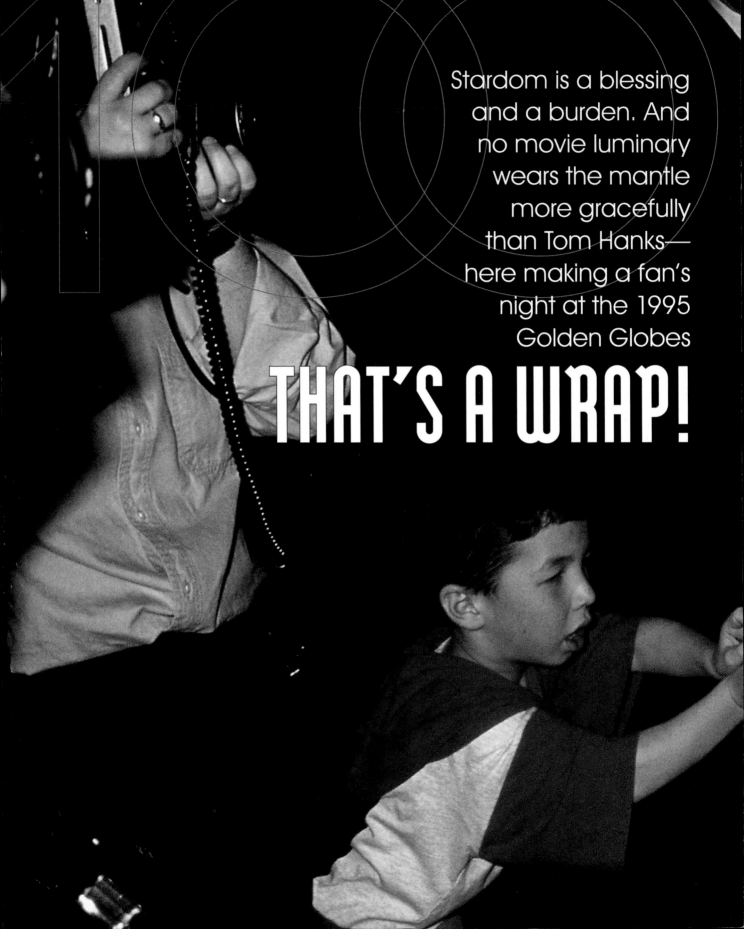

Stardom is a blessing
and a burden. And
no movie luminary
wears the mantle
more gracefully
than Tom Hanks—
here making a fan's
night at the 1995
Golden Globes

# THAT'S A WRAP!

# PICTURE CREDITS

## Front Cover
Timothy White/Corbis Outline
Insets, from left (softcover only):
George Pimental/London Features;
Marc Kayne/J.M.E.; Kobal Collection;
Douglas Kirkland/Corbis Outline

## Title Page
Gwendolen Cates/Corbis Sygma

## Table of Contents
2 (clockwise from left) Armando
Gallo/Retna Ltd.; Greg Gorman/Corbis
Outline; Anacleto Rapping/LA Times/
Retna Ltd.; Nigel Parry/CPI; Robert
Fleischauer/LaMoine; Douglas Kirkland/
Corbis Outline; Timothy White/Corbis
Outline; MPTV; Michael O'Neill/Corbis
Outline; Dorothy Low/Shooting Star;
3 Sam Jones/Corbis Outline

## Roll 'Em
4-5 Steve Schapiro/Timepix

## Icons
6-7 Sante D'Orazio/Corbis Outline; 8-9
Paramount Pictures; 10-11 Corbis Sygma;
E.J. Camp/Corbis Outline; 12-13 Lance
Staedler/Corbis Outline; Merrick Morton;
14-15 Michael O'Neill/Corbis Outline; 16-
17 Photofest; Everett Collection; 18-19
Eva Sereny/Corbis Sygma; Douglas
Kirkland/Corbis Outline; 20-21 Timothy
White/Corbis Outline

## Bombshells
22-23 Art Streiber/Icon Int'l.; 24-25
Steven Klein/Corbis Outline; 26-27 Albert
Sanchez/Corbis Outline; Douglas Kirk-
land/Corbis Outline; 28-29 Jim Cooper/
Retna Ltd.; 30-31 Columbia/Kerry Hayes/
MPTV; Bettina Rheims/Corbis Sygma;
32-33 Sante D'Orazio/Corbis Outline

## Heartthrobs
34-35 Sam Jones/Corbis Outline; 36-37
Jeff Katz/Getty Images; 38-39 Everett
Collection; Lynn Goldsmith/Corbis Outline; 40-41 Isabel Snyder/Corbis Outline;
42-43 Lance Staedler/Corbis Outline;
Peter Mountain/20th Century Fox

## Master Class
46-47 Greg Gorman/Corbis Outline; 48-
49 Vern Evans; 50-51 Dorothy Low/Shoot-

ing Star; Michael O'Neill/Corbis Outline;
52-53 Camera Press/Retna Ltd.; Nigel
Parry/CPI; 54-55 Terry O'Neill/Corbis
Sygma; Genaro Molina/LA Times/Retna
Ltd.; 56-57 Sante D'Orazio/Corbis
Outline; Robert Fleischauer/LaMoine

## Role Players
58-59 Terry O'Neill/Corbis Sygma; 60-61
Brigitte Lacombe; Karen Kuehn/Matrix;
62-63 Kobal Collection; Timothy White/
Corbis Outline; 64-65 Brigitte Lacombe;
Blake Little/Icon Int'l.; 66-67 Cliff Watts/
Icon Int'l.; Fergus Greer/Icon Int'l.; 68-69
Art Streiber/Icon Int'l.

## Double Threats
70-71 Tony Duran/Corbis Outline; Fred
Prouser/Reuters/Timepix; 72 Bill Eppridge/
Timepix; Everett Collection; 73 Ruven
Afanador/Corbis Outline; Martha Swope/
Timepix; 74-75 Michael Grecco/Icon Int'l.;
Todd Kaplan/Starfile; 76 MPTV; Douglas
Kirkland/Corbis Outline; 77 Douglas Kirk-
land/Corbis Outline; Lynn Goldsmith/Cor-
bis Outline; 78-79 Kevin Mazur/Wireimage
(inset); Harry Langdon; 80-81 Douglas
Kirkland/Corbis Outline; Bettman/Corbis

## Action Heroes
82-83 Kobal Collection; 84-85 Eddie
Adams/Corbis Outline; 86-87 Fergus
Greer/Icon Int'l.; Rafael Roa/Corbis Outline; 88-89; Anacleto Rapping/LA Times/
Retna Ltd.; Justin Case/Corbis Outline;
90-91 Kobal Collection; Fabrice Trum-
bert/Retna Ltd.; 92-93 Greg Gorman/
Corbis Outline

## America's Sweethearts
94-95 Francesco Escalar; 96-97 Kobal
Collection; Marouze Jean Claude/
Corbis Sygma; 98-99 Andrew Eccles/
Corbis Outline; Art Streiber/Icon Int'l.;
100-101 Timothy White/Corbis Outline;
Theodore Wood/Retna Ltd.; 102-103
Dana Fineman-Appel/Icon Int'l.

## The Wild Ones
104-105 Anne Marie Fox/Corbis Sygma;
106-107 Bob Frame/LaMoine; Danny
Rothenberg/Visages; 108-109 Anne Marie
Fox/Corbis/Sygma; 110-111 Robert Erd-
mann/Icon Int'l.; 112-113 Bill Reitzel/Corbis
Outline; Claudio Carpi/Corbis Outline

## Star Bursts
114-115 Orion/Warner Bros.; 116-117
Alan Pappe; Timothy Greenfield-
Sanders/Corbis Outline; 118-119
Douglas Kirkland/Corbis Outline;
120-121 Kobal Collection; Getty
Images; 122-123 Neil Leifer

## Clowns
124-125 Patrick Harbron; 126-127
Kirk McKoy/LA Times/Retna Ltd.;
Getty Images; 128-129 Timothy White/
Corbis Outline; 130-131 Sam Jones/
Corbis Outline; Myles Aronowitz/Everett
Collection; 132-133 Michael Grecco/
Icon Int'l.; 134-135 Geraint Lewis/Corbis
Sygma; Stephen Danelian/Corbis Out-
line; 136-137 Gwendolen Cates/Icon
Int'l.; Alan Levenson; 138-139 Gwendolen
Cates/CPI

## That's a Wrap!
140-141 Vinnie Zuffante/Starfile

## Back Cover
Row 1: (Affleck) Anacleto Rapping/
LA Times/Retna Ltd.; (Kidman) Albert
Sanchez/Corbis Outline; (Brando) Merrick
Morton; (Diaz) Theodore Wood/Retna Ltd.;
(Washington) E.J. Camp/Corbis Outline
Row 2: (Cher) Harry Langdon; (Clooney)
Sam Jones/Corbis Outline; (Lopez) Tony
Duran/Corbis Outline; (Newman) MPTV;
(Foster) Lance Staedler/Corbis Outline
Row 3: (Ford) Timothy White/Corbis Out-
line; (Ryan) Francesco Escalar; (Smith)
Michael Grecco/Icon Int'l.; (Zeta-Jones)
Jim Cooper/Retna Ltd.; (Di Caprio) Peter
Mountain/20th Century Fox
Row 4: (Moore) Kerry Hayes/Columbia/
MPTV; (Redford) Photofest; (Streisand)
Bill Eppridge/Timepix; (Gibson) Jeff Katz/
Getty Images; (Pfeiffer) Sante D'Orazio/
Corbis Outline
Row 5: (Beatty) Eva Sereny/Corbis Sygma
(softcover only); (Basinger) Steven Klein/
Corbis Outline; (Connery) Rafael Roa/
Corbis Outline; (Barrymore) Art Streiber/
Icon Int'l.; (Jackson) Claudio Carpi/
Corbis Outline

# INDEX